SOCIAL

Other interview books from Automatic Press ♦ $\frac{\vee}{!}$ P

Formal Philosophy
edited by Vincent F. Hendricks & John Symons November 2005

Masses of Formal Philosophy
edited by Vincent F. Hendricks & John Symons October 2006

Philosophy of Technology: 5 Questions
edited by Jan-Kyrre Berg Olsen & Evan Selinger February 2007

Game Theory: 5 Questions
edited by Vincent F. Hendricks & Pelle Guldborg Hansen April 2007

Philosophy of Mathematics: 5 Questions
edited by Vincent F. Hendricks & Hannes Leitgeb January 2008

Philosophy of Computing and Information: 5 Questions
edited by Luciano Floridi Sepetmber 2008

Epistemology: 5 Questions
edited by Vincent F. Hendricks & Duncan Pritchard September 2008

Philosophy of Medicine: 5 Questions
edited by J. K. B. O. Friis, P. Rossel & M. S. Norup September 2011

Narrative Theories and Poetics: 5 Questions
edited by Peer F. Bundbaard, Henrik Skov Nielsen & Frederik Stjernfelt 2012

Intellectual History: 5 Questions
edited by Morten Haugaard Jeppesen, Frederik Stjernfelt & Mikkel Thorup May 2013

Philosophical Practice: 5 Questions
edited by Jeanette Bresson Ladegaard Knox & Jan Kyrre Berg Olsen Friis January 2013

Philosophy of Nursing: 5 Questions
edited by Anette Forss, Christine Ceci & John S. Drummod October 2014

Science and Religion: 5 Questions
edited by Gregg D. Caruso March 2014

Peirce: 5 Questions
edited by Francesco Bellucci, Ahti-Veikko Pietarinen & Frederik Stjernfelt July 2014

See all published and forthcoming books in the 5 Questions series at www. vince-inc. com

SOCIAL EPISTEMOLOGY:
5 QUESTIONS

EDITED BY

VINCENT F. HENDRICKS

DUNCAN PRITCHARD

Automatic Press ♦ $\frac{\text{V}}{\text{I}}$ P

Automatic Press ♦ $\frac{V}{I}$ P

Information on this title: www. vince-inc. com

© Automatic Press / VIP 2015

First published 2015

Printed in the United States of America
and the United Kingdom

ISBN-13 / 978-87-92130-53-2

Cover design by Vincent F. Hendricks

Contents

Preface

———————————— ◆ ————————————

Social Epistemology: 5 Questions is a collection of interviews with some of the world's most influential scholars working on social epistemology, from a range of disciplinary perspectives (e.g., sociology, computer science, philosophy, political theory, behavioral science). We hear their views on social epistemology; its aim, scope, use, broader intellectual environment, future direction, and how the work of the interviewees fits in these respects. Given the huge growth of research in this field over the last few years, this collection presents a fascinating insight into the current state-of-play in this area, and also offers an intriguing account of how this field might develop in the future.

Vincent F. Hendricks & Duncan Pritchard
Copenhagen & Edinburgh
November 2014

1

David Bloor

Professor Emeritus

Science Studies Unit, University of Edinburgh

I must begin by begging the readers' (and the editors') indulgence. I want to make a change in the wording of the five editorial questions. I want to substitute the words 'sociology of knowledge' for 'social epistemology'. Thus I shall read the first question as asking why I was initially drawn to the sociology of knowledge, and so on throughout the remaining queries. There are two reasons for making such a change. The first is, admittedly, subjective. The label 'social epistemology' feels alien because I do not routinely use this label to describe my own work. I always say that I am trying to contribute to the sociology of knowledge and, in particular, the sociology of scientific knowledge. The second reason touches on something more objective. Such labels are not matters of arbitrary notation but carry information about methodological allegiances and intellectual alliances. I prefer the label 'sociology of knowledge' because it better conveys the tradition of work on which I draw and the models, methods and paradigms that inform the way I proceed. With these provisos in mind I shall now address the set questions.

1. Why were you initially drawn to social epistemology?

I was first drawn to the sociology of knowledge in the late 1960s through the work and influence of two of my colleagues in the Science Studies Unit in the University of Edinburgh. The colleagues in question were Barry Barnes, who had originally been a chemist but who had converted to sociology, and Steven Shapin, who had been a biologist but who had become an historian of science[1]. The remit of the newly created

---

[1] Some idea of the work of Barnes and Shapin can be gathered from the following small selection of their publications: B. Barnes, *Scientific Knowledge and Sociological Theory*, London, Routledge and Kegan Paul, 1974. B. Barnes, *T.S. Kuhn and Social Science*, London, Macmillan, 1982. B. Barnes, *About Science*, Oxford, Blackwell, 1985. S. Shapin and S. Schaffer, *Leviathan and the Air-Pump. Hobbes, Boyle and he Experimental Life*, Princeton, Princeton University Press, 1985. S. Shapin, *A Social History of Truth. Civility and Science in Seventeenth-Century England*, Chicago, Chicago University Press, 1994. S. Shapin, *The Scientific Life. A Moral History of a Late Modern Vocation*, Chicago, University of Chicago

Unit was to offer courses to science and engineering students with the aim of broadening their education. The general theme was 'science and society' but since the enterprise was a novel one there was no existing syllabus or disciplinary tradition. We had the freedom to invent the content of 'science studies' as we went along[2].

Our solution to this problem naturally drew on the resources of existing work in a number of fields but we soon converged on what was recognisably a version of the sociology of knowledge. As we understood that enterprise it was based on the empirical case-studies of historians, sociologists and anthropologists. Its theoretical content was thus to be disciplined by empirical and explanatory concerns. The aim was to treat knowledge as a naturally occurring phenomenon which was located in space and time and grounded in the causal processes of the natural world. Individual knowing subjects and their cultures were part of this natural realm. The institution of science was to be seen as a collective, cultural achievement.

My own trajectory towards the sociological stance was via training in experimental psychology in the University of Cambridge. I was, and still am, drawn to the idea of a scientific analysis of knowledge and, initially, experimental psychology seemed to provide the desired analysis. My intellectual heroes were Frederick Bartlett, Donald Broadbent and Richard Gregory. I was fortunate to be able to attend lectures by Broadbent and Gregory at Cambridge. Bartlett had retired but still had an office in the Applied Psychology Unit. Bartlett's classic book *Remembering. A Study in Experimental and Social Psychology* had been published in 1932 but was still required reading when I was a student in the mid 60s[3]. To me the book was a revelation and it bridged the gap between the psychological and the social. Bartlett developed a position that he called 'social constructiveness' and even applied that approach to examples drawn from science and technology. It was only in retrospect that I became fully aware of just how much I had imbibed from Bartlett but, beyond doubt, all of this served to make me receptive to the broader perspective offered by the sociology and history of science that I learned about from my new Edinburgh colleagues. For me the sociology of knowledge was a generalisation of the perspective taught

---

Press, 2008.

[2] The Science Studies Unit was part of the Faculty of Science and its foundation was a response to government reports calling for the improvement of scientific education. See R.M. Birse, *Science at the University of Edinburgh: 1583-1993*, Edinburgh, University of Edinburgh, 1994, 165-166.

[3] F. Bartlett, *Remembering. A Study in Experimental and Social Psychology*, Cambridge, C.U.P., 1932.

by the impressive and hard-headed experimentalists in the psychology laboratory in Cambridge[4].

2. What are your main contributions to the field of social epistemology?

I must confess to an abiding naivety about the academic world. One expression of this failing is that I assumed that the excitement of developing a sociological account of scientific knowledge would be shared by others outside the Science Studies Unit. I foolishly believed that a scientific approach to the nature of scientific knowledge would seem intrinsically attractive and interesting to any scholars with a professional interest in the status and character of knowledge. It was a shock to realise that, rather than being welcomed, such an approach is widely seen as an attack on science and an endorsement of irrationalism[5].

These criticisms raise a number of questions which, themselves, belong to the sociology of knowledge though I do not pretend to know the answers to them. The reaction suggests that the intellectual climate must have changed between the 1930s, when Bartlett published his work on social constructiveness, and the 1960s and 70s when we, at the Science Studies Unit, began publishing our papers. Bartlett had not been attacked as anti-scientific. On the contrary, he was honoured as a Fellow of the Royal Society of London. Those who, today, sneer at social constructivism should ponder this fact. Those who think that social constructivism is the product of 'post-modernism' should think again[6].

It is not social constructiveness that has changed since Bartlett's day: it is a section of the audience for such work that has chosen to become hostile and vocal[7]. All too often the facts and arguments presented in the

---

[4] D. Bloor, 'Whatever happened to social constructiveness?', in A. Saito (ed.), *Bartlett, Culture and Cognition*, London, Psychology Press, 2000, 194-215.

[5] In his 2006 article on social epistemology, in the on-line *Stanford Encyclopaedia of Philosophy*, Alvin Goldman repeatedly, and wrongly, insists that members of the 'Edinburgh School' are engaged in 'debunking' science. Our denial that this is either the aim or consequence of our work is dismissed as 'disingenuous'.

[6] Like most scientists, Bartlett was an instinctive materialist. His social constructivism was not a form of philosophical idealism. There is, however, a tendency in the critical literature (as in Goldman's article cited above) to assume that social constructivism is idealist and that any version which is not idealist can be dismissed as 'weak' or 'innocuous'. Thus the position is only deemed 'interesting' if it is also wholly implausible – so that it can be conveniently dismissed. Another rhetorical move frequently made by critics is to link together fundamentally different positions, e.g. the writings of Bruno Latour are discussed alongside those of the strong program. For the differences see D. Bloor, 'Anti-Latour', *Studies in History and Philosophy of Science*, 30, 1999, 81-112.

[7] A similar shift has occurred with regard to relativism. For a discussion of some of the ideological complexities of these arguments see D. Bloor, 'Relativism and the

course of a sociological analysis are simply passed over by the critics and replaced by the imputation of unworthy, anti-scientific, motives. I have spent much of my professional life attempting to explain what is wrong with these critical reactions. For example, critics say that sociologists have failed to do justice to the reasons advanced by scientists and insist that these reasons must be 'disentangled' from what is social. In making this response the critics show that they have failed to appreciate the central thrust of the sociological argument: namely, that reasons are social phenomena and operate as part of a causal nexus. To try to disentangle the rational from the social would be like trying to 'disentangle' the wool from a knitted garment[8].

To meet the criticisms directed at the sociology of knowledge I attempted to codify the principles that informed the excellent scholarship of those who were trying to furnish accurate and factual descriptions of scientific practice. This scholarship was primarily, though not exclusively, the product of historians of science. These historians were not telling us what they thought science ought to be but were engaged in the much more important task of saying what it actually was. I called the resulting codification of the historians' methods of investigation by the name of 'the strong program' in the sociology of knowledge[9]. The program itself was more descriptive than prescriptive. The aim was not to tell historians what to do (they did not need to be told). It was to tell others what was already being done in order to help defend this valuable enterprise from misunderstanding.

Such defensive work is necessary but it can never be fully satisfying. The work which gives more satisfaction, and which is intrinsically more important for the discipline, is positive and empirical. My greatest pleasure has come from the years I have spent researching an historical case study. This research has recently culminated in *The Enigma of the Aerofoil. Rival Theories in Aerodynamics 1909-1930*. The book contains a sociological analysis of a long-standing controversy about

Sociology of Scientific Knowledge' in S.D. Hales (ed.), *A Companion to Relativism*, Oxford, Blackwell, 2011, 433-455.

[8]   The call to 'disentangle' the rational and the social comes from Dudley Shapere. The argument showing the ultimate futility of the demand comes from Wittgenstein's analysis of rule following. Unfortunately that argument is frequently misunderstood, see: D. Bloor, *Wittgenstein: Rules and Institutions*, London, Routledge, 1997.

[9]   D. Bloor, 'Wittgenstein and Mannheim on the Sociology of Mathematics', *Studies in History and Philosophy of Science*, 4, 1973, 173-191. D. Bloor, *Knowledge and Social Imagery*, London, Routledge and Kegan Paul, 1976 (2nd edn., University of Chicago Press, 1991).

the operation of an aircraft wing and the reasons why the wing generates lift. The rival accounts of lift involve disputes in the realm of fluid
dynamics, and the sociological analysis necessarily engages with the
scientific reasoning of the relevant experts. The argument of the book is
therefore somewhat technical but it has its lighter moments. It provided
me with an occasion to confront the over-confident critics of social constructivism who think that they can refute it simply by pointing out that
aeroplanes fly. The critics are badly wrong. The science of aerodynamics provides a particularly good field for demonstrating the strengths
of social constructivism although this will only be apparent to those
who take the trouble to acquaint themselves with the facts of the case[10].

3. What is the proper role of social epistemology in relation to other disciplines?

The sociology of knowledge stands in two sorts of relationship to work
in other disciplines. In one case these other disciplines provide *topics* of
research; in the other case they provide *resources* for the conduct of the
research. As in the example I have just given, a subject such as aerodynamics can be a topic of sociological research. Other subjects, such as
experimental psychology, might provide resources that sociologists can
appeal to in the course of their analysis. For example, Bartlett's work on
remembering identifies and illuminates a process called 'conventionali-
sation' that takes place when an element from one culture is assimilated
into another culture. I use Bartlett's work in my analysis of the history
of aerodynamics when I described the way in which the work of a British engineer, Frederick Lanchester, was understood (or misunderstood)
by Cambridge mathematicians.

It is worth stating this point about resources in its full generality. Sociology is but one strand of a naturalistic analysis of knowledge. There
are a range of different disciplines which must contribute to any adequate, this-worldly, causal account of knowledge. There can be no such
thing as a 'purely' sociological analysis of knowledge, any more than
there can be a 'purely' psychological account or a 'purely' neurological
account. Sociologists, like all these other specialists, are respectively
contributing but one element to the future, overall picture of cognition.
Because human knowledge is a shared achievement, and a socially sustained collective good, the sociologist knows that there will always be
a sociological element. The 'strength' referred to in the label 'strong
program' lies precisely in this claim: that there can be no fully-fledged

---

[10] D. Bloor, *The Enigma of the Aerofoil. Rival Theories in Aerodynamics 1909-1930*, Chicago, University of Chicago Press, 2011.

human knowledge, such as science, which falls outside the legitimate scope of sociological enquiry.

An interesting special case is the relation that the sociology of knowledge bears to itself. In principle the sociology of knowledge is both a topic and a resource. This is why the strong program contained a principle of 'reflexivity'. No sociologist of knowledge can consistently take the view that the knowledge of others must be sociologically explicable while his or her own knowledge is exempt from the causal processes found elsewhere.

Reflexivity has long been seen by critics as giving rise to a form of self-contradiction, but those who level this charge are begging the question. They are assuming that sociological causation implies the falsity of a knowledge claim. This premise is, of course, rejected by sociologists of knowledge, but it is worth asking why the critic's inference from social causation to falsity sometimes seems plausible. The answer is because of the widespread, but mistaken, belief that the sociologist is saying that knowledge is a response to society *rather than* a response to the natural world. But this is not what sociologists of knowledge are saying. They are saying that interaction with the material world is a reality but the interaction is a collective interaction. The social collectivity is not an impediment to contact with material reality, rather, it is the medium which facilitates and gives meaning to that contact.

4. What have been the most significant advances in social epistemology?

The most significant recent advances in the sociology of scientific knowledge have taken the form of two theoretical insights. Both of these insights have been impressively developed by my Edinburgh colleague Barry Barnes. The first insight is the position called 'meaning finitism'; the second is the 'self-referential' (or 'performative') model of social institutions.

Meaning finitism is the claim that each act of concept application is problematic and is a proper object of sociological curiosity and explanation. Every concept must be introduced ostensively or defined in terms that have been introduced ostensively. For every such concept the number of exemplars by which it is taught must be finite. The move from the finite number of exemplars to the next case is under-determined by previous applications. Past application are but one of the contingencies impinging on the step to the next case. The full range of contextual factors, from sensory inputs to current goals and interests, must be taken into account in any causal analysis[11].

Meaning finitism provides the answer to attacks on relativism of the kind proposed by John Searle. Searle accepts that definitions are relative in all manner of ways but he argues that, once meanings have been fixed by definitions, the fulfilment of the satisfaction conditions that have been laid down, or the failure to fulfil them, is "no longer a matter of any kind of relativism". It is determined by the material world and, by implication, is to be taken as an absolute thing. But if meaning finitism is right, Searle is wrong to think of meanings as things which can be 'fixed'. The premise of his argument against relativism is false[12].

The self-referential model of institutions expresses the idea that social entities are created by the references that are made to them. Thus when person A refers to, say, the property of being 'money' or the property of being the 'leader', A's reference is actually a reference to the acts of reference by persons B, C, D etc to money or leadership. And the same is true for the references made by B, C or D. Stated simply, money is money because it is called money and a leader is the leader in virtue of being called the leader. Of course, 'being called' stands duty for all manner of verbal and non-verbal forms of orientation, acknowledgement, invoking, etc. The central point is that discourse about social entities does not have an object that is independent of that discourse. Here, then, is a simple but potentially profound theory of social ontology. At first glance the theory seems to reduce social reality to a mere matter of talk. It is proper to ask if the theory can do justice to the harsh reality of social life with its unequal distribution of power, freedom and material resources. The answer is that it can, and Barnes has developed these ideas in an important book called *The Nature of Power*[13].

5. What are the most important open problems in social epistemology and what are the prospects for progress?

In the developing field of the sociology of knowledge there are many unsolved, technical problems that await empirical and conceptual clarification. For example, there are psychological mechanisms that must

[11] For a development of meaning finitism see B. Barnes, D. Bloor and J. Henry, *Scientific Knowledge. A Sociological Analysis*, Chicago, University of Chicago Press, 1996.

[12] J. Searle, *The Construction of Social Reality*, London, Allen Lane, 1995, p. 166.

[13] For the first statement of the theory see B. Barnes, 'Social Life as Bootstrapped Induction', *Sociology*, vol. 17, No. 4, 1983, 524-545. For its further development see B. Barnes, *The Nature of Power*, Cambridge, Polity Press, 1988. Barnes' position must not be confused with Searle's in *The Construction of Social Reality*. For Searle the self-reference resides in the content of individual mental states.

underpin what, in everyday parlance, is called 'paying attention to something,' 'intending something' and 'meaning something'. These mechanisms must stand in an intimate relation to the processes of social interaction which give an objective, normative structure (and hence, propositional content) to these, otherwise, subjective individual processes. This relation badly needs further exploration. It is vital for understanding how the self-referential processes, central to Barnes' model of institutions, can be set in motion. But, urgent though it is to clarify such matters, the open question I want to address here is of a more general kind.

I want to consider the relation between the sociology of scientific knowledge and the philosophy of science. If 'epistemology' is defined simply as 'the theory of knowledge' then the sociology of knowledge could reasonably be brought under the rubric of social epistemology. But, as the word 'epistemology' is typically used, it refers to a branch of philosophy and epistemological questions are thought of as characteristically 'philosophical' in nature. What, then, is the relation between the sociological analysis of knowledge and the analysis of knowledge offered by philosophers? Are their accounts in competition with one another or are they capable of co-existing side-by-side?

An answer frequently proposed by philosophers is that the tasks of the two disciplines should be seen as complementary. A division of labour is suggested which hinges on the distinction between 'is' and 'ought'. Sociologists, aspiring to be empirical scientists, should deal with factual questions about the beliefs, inferences and practices of social actors, while philosophers deal with evaluative questions. Thus, the argument goes, sociologist will describe and causally explain beliefs in terms of their psycho-social determinants while philosophers will concern themselves with their rational justification and their truth and falsity. As one philosopher of science put it: Philosophers "take reflective responsibility, as it were, for the normativity of our most fundamental cognitive categories"[14].

This proposal may be illustrated by an example drawn from my study of aerodynamics. In his treatise *Hydrodynamics*, the mathematician Horace Lamb treated the Euler equations as describing the flow of an unreal, 'perfect' fluid. By contrast Lamb treated the Stokes equations as providing a true account of the real-world phenomenon of viscous flow.

---

[14] M. Friedman, 'On the sociology of scientific knowledge and its philosophical agenda', *Studies in History and Philosophy of Science*, 29, 1998, 239-271.

Lamb was confident that the empirical evidence justified this distinction. Lamb's position was very different to that of his younger contemporary Richard von Mises who treated both the Euler and the Stokes equations as 'abstractions'. Both sets of equations, said von Mises, are instruments for dealing with reality but in neither case did they amount to a representation of a real fluid[15].

Here, in simple form, is a divergence of judgement of the sort that attracts the attention of both philosophers and sociologists. Sociologists will note the difference and try to explain it. They may seek to shed light on the difference by noting that Lamb was a Cambridge mathematical physicist while von Mises was a central-European engineer. The two men belonged to different intellectual traditions and this may help explain their different positions and their divergent methodological judgements. A philosopher, by contrast, would want to clarify what was meant by the notions of 'truth' and 'abstraction' that were used by these experts and would want to address the question of which one of them, Lamb or von Mises, had the right view of the status of the Stokes equations.

The two sets of questions posed above, the one factual the other evaluative, are both legitimate. That is to say: there are contexts in which they are legitimate. But do they correspond to and support the division of labour that has been proposed between the philosopher and the sociologist? I think there are grounds for doubting that the difference between the questions is sufficient to demarcate two, genuine, disciplinary perspectives and hence justify the idea that epistemology can exist in parallel to the sociology of knowledge.

Consider the task of clarification. Clarification is a pragmatic activity that is always to be understood and assessed relative to the goals and interests of those seeking clarification. It is also an activity that only makes sense relative to the current state of knowledge in the region of the puzzle. The process of clarification will assume different forms and invoke different criteria in different fields and at different times. The only persons in a position to offer useful clarifications (that is, genuine clarifications) are those who are immersed in, and answerable to, the specialist requirements of particular disciplines. The attempt to sustain an academic discipline which specialises in 'clarification' as such, and

---

[15] H. Lamb, *Hydrodynamics*, Cambridge, C.U.P., 1932, p.575. The respective positions of Lamb and von Mises are discussed in chapter five of *The Enigma of the Aerofoil*. See note 10.

which generates its own norms of clarity, is something else again, and is wholly unrealistic.

The same problems arise with normative assessments of a more general kind. Some such assessments are integral to every organised, cognitive activity. Thus, von Mises was implicitly, and sometimes explicitly, evaluating Lamb's stance. The right of von Mises is clear; that of the philosopher is not. In some sense, everyone has a right to an opinion, but not everyone can speak with authority or reasonably expect that their conclusions carry credibility. (If philosophers simply echo authorities that are already accepted then the authority the philosopher seems to possess is merely derivative and philosophy becomes an exercise in public relations or ideology or propaganda.) So the question is: How did philosophers earn their self-proclaimed status as the guardians of "our" most fundamental cognitive categories? I have never heard a plausible answer to this question.

It might be objected that these sociological reflections on the relative character of conceptual clarification, and the socially located character of normative authority, are themselves of a 'philosophical' nature. In raising questions about the nature of philosophy am I not myself doing philosophy? Such an argument should be viewed with suspicion. It is like the argument that is sometimes proposed by religious believers. These believers insist that unbelievers, who say that God does not exist, are themselves making theological statements – and are therefore showing that theology is, after all, a legitimate activity.

A better argument might be the following. Sociologists and psychologists make use of the work of philosophers when they are trying to build their scientific accounts of knowledge. No one who reads Edwin Boring's *History of Experimental Psychology* can doubt the contribution of figures such as Locke, Berkeley, Mill and Bain to the growth of this empirical discipline[16]. Again, didn't Durkheim grapple with Kant when he wrote his *Elementary Forms of the Religious Life*?[17] Such facts surely show that naturalistic disciplines concerned with cognition have philosophical roots and rest upon presuppositions extracted, rightly or wrongly, from the work of philosophers. Doesn't this suggest that philosophers have a right to be called in to monitor such borrowings and assess their wisdom, or lack of wisdom?

---

[16] E.G. Boring, *A History of Experimental Psychology*, New York, Appleton-Century-Crofts, 1950.

[17] Emile Durkheim, *The Elementary Forms of the Religious Life*, trans. J.W. Swain, New York, Collier Books, 1961. First published 1912.

In my own work I borrow insights from writers who are now counted as 'philosophers', e.g. David Hume, Ludwig Wittgenstein, and Mary Hesse (who was one of my own teachers). I therefore grant the facts on which the above argument is based, but I want to challenge the conclusions drawn from these facts. The picture on which the argument depends is of the practitioners of empirical disciplines helping themselves to arguments which are properly called 'philosophical'. But we can also see the situation as one in which, what is currently called 'philosophy', is a patchwork containing elements which really belong to a range of empirical sciences: some to psychology, some to sociology and others to yet other sciences. I therefore propose a Gestalt switch in which the allegedly 'philosophical' elements of the empirical sciences are reconfigured as scientific elements that are improperly imprisoned within the would-be discipline called 'philosophy'.

There is an old criticism of philosophy in which it is dismissed as 'armchair' psychology or 'armchair' sociology. I sympathise with this argument but I am not wholly dismissing philosophy: I am trying to rescue something from it. I am saying that there are valuable, theoretical resources to be retrieved. They should be cherished and relocated in the disciplines that can best carry them forward. The residue may then be discarded. Thus Locke, Berkeley, Mill and Bain were doing associationist psychology. Hume's account of conventions and the problem of collective action (as it would now be called) was theoretical sociology of the highest order. When Kant invoked the noumenal machinery of the categories he was unwittingly engaging in transfigured talk about the social character of knowledge – as Durkheim pointed out. Wittgenstein offered a penetrating, reductive, sociological analysis of rule-following, while Hesse's account of scientific inference laid the foundation for the finitist account of meaning[18]. But what is, and is not, valuable in these contributions, and how they should be interpreted, is for the psychologist and the sociologist to decide.

It will now be apparent why I see myself as contributing to the sociology of knowledge rather than social epistemology. Social epistemology is philosophy and the status of philosophy, as an academic discipline, is deeply problematic. I do not think that the sciences, whether natural or social, possess (or need) anything that should be called 'philosophical' foundations. In as far as any body of human knowledge has foundations at all they are causal foundations, that is, they are biological, psychological and sociological in character and should be studied as biological,

---

[18] M. Hesse, *The Structure of Scientific Inference*, London, Macmillan, 1974.

psychological and sociological phenomena. This is the ultimate reason for my terminological intransigence regarding the label 'social epistemology'. I take the view that social epistemology is the sociology of knowledge – or it is nothing.

2

Richard Bradley

Professor of Philosophy

London School of Economics and Political Science

---

1. Why were you initially drawn to social epistemology?

I have a long standing interest in the sociology and politics of knowledge, going back to my undergraduate years as a social sciences student. Indeed I originally intended to do my doctoral dissertation on the topic of ideology, before being seduced away by the elegance and explanatory power of modern decision theory. My interest in what Alvin Goldman calls veritistic social epistemology[1] is much more recent however and grew out of my research in belief revision and formation on the one hand and into group decision making on the other. Discovering Keith Lehrer and Carl Wagner's book *Rational Consensus in Science and Society*[2] was an inspiring moment for me, because it gave me some idea of what could be achieved by modeling social epistemic processes formally.

Approaching social epistemology from group decision making has coloured my view of the field, for better or worse. One beneficial effect has been that certain questions arise naturally from this perspective, such as those relating to the role that social epistemic mechanisms can play in helping groups make good decisions, which might not immediately occur to someone coming from traditional individualistic epistemology.

2. What are your main contributions to the field of social epistemology?

My main contribution (and I am by no means unique in doing this) has been to apply the techniques of formal epistemology and decision theory to problems in social epistemology. Most of my work has been on

---

[1] Goldman, A (1999) *Knowledge in a Social World*, Oxford: Oxford University Press

[2] Lehrer, K and C. Wagner (1981) *Rational Consensus in Science and Society*, Dordrecht: Reidel

the properties of different social mechanisms for establishing a consensus on what to do, what to believe and what to value, and on the nature of the consensus achieved thereby. I'll give two examples that are interesting not so much for the particular results associated with them, but for the way they demonstrate how application of formal methods can not only help address questions in social epistemology in a relatively precise way, but also help to suggest new questions.

Firstly, inspired by some earlier work of Christian List[3], I have been looking at the epistemic virtues (and vices) of different voting systems for deciding questions that admit of true or false answers, e.g. whether some particular candidate is the most suited for a job or whether the accused is guilty of the crime. Voting systems have interesting epistemic properties, as Condorcet famously demonstrated through what is now known as the Condorcet Jury theorem. One crucial issue, for instance, is the reliability of different voting systems (and social epistemic mechanisms more generally) with regard to producing true answers to such questions. A good mechanism will exploit the knowledge held by the individuals making up the group however the knowledge is distributed and whatever its extent. As Condorcet's theorem shows, majority rule does this well if most individuals are reasonably competent on the questions on which they are voting, poorly if they are not. A rule which I have studied quite extensively together with Christopher Thompson – multiple vote majority rule – does much better across a range of profiles of individual competence as long as we are assuming that individuals are interested only in the truth and vote non-strategically.[4] Indeed it does almost as well as rules which weight the voting power of individuals according to their competence on the issue at hand, and is far less 'demanding' both informationally, in that it does not require that individual competences be known, and normatively, in that it preserves the idea of equal participation in decision making on the part of individuals.

Secondly, I have been examining different ways of organizing deliberation within groups and assessing their properties[5]. There has been a

[3]   List, C. (2008) "Distributed Cognition: A Perspective from Social Choice Theory", in M. Albert, D. Schmidtchen and S. Voigt (eds.), *Scientific Competition: Theory and Policy*, Conferences on New Political Economy vol. 24, Tuebingen (Mohr Siebeck), 2008

[4]   Bradley, R. and C. Thompson (2012) A (Mainly Epistemic) Argument for Multiple-vote Majority Rule http://personal.lse.ac.uk/bradleyr/pdf/MVMR%20 (Episteme).pdf , Episteme, 9: 63 - 79

[5]   See, for instance, Bradley, R (2006) *Taking Advantage of Difference of Opinion*, Episteme, 3 (3): 141-155

good deal of debate in political theory and philosophy over the merits of deliberation as a means of establishing a consensus, both normatively and epistemically. On the whole, however, this discussion has been hampered by the absence of a framework and set of corresponding tools for examining claims about the performance of deliberation on these dimensions relative to other mechanisms that might be used. What my work does, I think, is provide some of the tools required for epistemic assessment, so that much more nuanced answers can be given to questions of performance. For, as one might expect, how good deliberation is at delivering the right sort of consensus depends not only on the criteria for 'good' and 'right' but also on the exact nature of the deliberative mechanism employed, how information is distributed amongst individuals, what their incentives are, and so on.

3. What is the proper role of social epistemology in relation to other disciplines?

Social epistemology has already established itself as a recognised subfield of epistemology, but if it remains just that I would be a bit disappointed. We should, it seems to me, make epistemology as a whole more thoroughly social in its outlook rather than just develop social epistemology as a standalone field.

Social epistemology has a particularly significant role to play in relation both to the social sciences and to social choice and public policy, because the production of specific types of knowledge plays an important role in the functioning of social institutions and the conduct of collective projects. There is scope here for contributions both to the explanation of social institutions and projects (in a descriptive social epistemology) and to their design (in a normative one). Philip Kitcher's recollection of Marx, is particularly apt here:

> "How do we best design social institutions for the advancement of learning? The philosophers have ignored the social structure of science. The point, however, is to change it."[6]

Kitcher's claim is applicable not just to science, but also to institutions whose aims, though different from that of science, nonetheless depend for their fulfillment on the availability of specific epistemic goods. Law

---

[6] Kitcher, P. (1990) "The Division of Cognitive Labour" *Journal of Philosophy*, Vol. 87 (1): 5-22

provides a good example, because its proper functioning depends on different individuals and groups (the judge and the jury, for instance) producing judgements that are true, accurate, reliable, and/or appropriate at various points in the legal process. So here there is much scope for social epistemologists to act not only as social scientists but also as social reformers.

4. What have been the most significant advances in social epistemology?

There have been two critical phases of innovation in social epistemology. The first came when Marx, Mannheim and others made knowledge and belief itself an object of study, specifically social scientific study. Two very important ideas came out of their work: firstly that social position is a causal factor in determining what individuals believe, and secondly, that what individuals believe contributes to the stability (or otherwise) of social systems by serving to legitimate it or the practices associated with it. On the downside, they never delivered a detailed account of the mechanisms by which this occurs - for instance, of how ideology works on the individual mind – and to some degree remained rather unclear as to whether these mechanisms served to distort reality, reveal it or to create it.

The second important innovation was the turn to an explicitly normative social epistemology, associated above all with the work of Alvin Goldman in the 1970s, which undertakes the evaluation of social practices in terms of their capacity to promote the achievement of epistemic goods such as knowledge or shared belief. Apart from its important impact on epistemology itself, this innovation opened up a whole new field of enquiry – the properties of social epistemic processes, conceived of as mechanisms for the production of epistemic goods – and the corresponding possibility of applications in the engineering of social institutions.

I should say that that I don't regard these two research programmes – the sociology of knowledge and normative social epistemology - as being in opposition to one another. Although the former tradition has been associated primarily with a 'hermeneutics of suspicion' which seeks to unmask the real interests underlying truth-claims, it could equally well be directed at the question of the social conditions required for the production of knowledge. Conversely a normative social epistemology can equally enquire into the conditions promoting the realization of social interest-relative epistemic goals of one kind or another.

5. What are the most important open problems in social epistemology and what are the prospects for progress?

Social epistemology is still an 'immature' discipline and not enough agreement has been established on basic terms and questions for it to be possible to give a list of open problems that would reflect every social epistemologist's view of the field. Putting it more positively, there are so many interesting lines of enquiry being pursued at the moment that any list is likely to become outdated as soon as it was written.

This being said, here is my idiosyncratic view of the field. Peer disagreement has received a lot of air time recently and I think it is fair to say that it is still an open question as to the right way to respond to differences of opinion. Progress here is most likely to come from a better understanding of the possible determinants of disagreement, including the incentives underlying the adoption of opinions. Doing so is of some practical importance because disagreement of amongst experts is a fact of life and a source of difficulty in formulating public policy. Indeed on it depends an important issue in the arrangement of deliberation; namely whether disagreement is productive (and therefore to be encouraged) or something that needs to be overcome.

A second important and open question, to my mind, concerns the goals of social epistemic mechanisms: knowledge, shared or common knowledge, or a belief and/or value consensus on those matters required for fruitful co-existence. These goals are sometimes in tension with one another. For example, when a consensus on some matter is 'spurious' in the sense that each individuals agreement with it is based on quite different reasons, than an increase in shared knowledge can dissolve the consensus. So we have to take a view on how these goals are to be weighed and reconciled.

Many of the interesting open questions in the field are connected with the design of optimal epistemic mechanisms. We currently know a great deal about aggregative mechanisms and even about their epistemic properties, but are really only at the beginnings of an understanding of how other mechanisms – including deliberation, prediction markets, and social search mechanisms - work and how they compare in terms of their conduciveness to accurate or true judgement on the part of individuals and collectives.

Similarly, although economics gives us a general theory of organization of production and in particular of the role of the division of labour, the application of these tools to the production of knowledge is still in its infancy. Different types of social organizations require different kinds of epistemic inputs, of different qualities and for different purposes. Compare for instance how knowledge and belief are produced and regulated in legal proceedings – through rules of evidence, standards for judgements, criteria for jury selection, and so on – with how they are produced and used in public policy formation – through committees, focus groups, planning boards, and so on, intertwining democratic consultation with the contributions of experts.

Significant progress on these questions – both explanatory and normative – is most likely to be obtained if, and only if, there is something of an interdisciplinary focus on them. My feeling is that many of the tools are already available but that a concerted effort needs to be made to bring them together in joint research projects involving researchers in both philosophy and the social sciences. If that were done, then social epistemology could be part of a new philosophy of society that was as fertile as the philosophies of mind, language and cognition have been in recent decades.

3

Cristina Bicchieri

S. J. Patterson Harvie Professor of Philosophy and Psychology
University of Pennsylvania

1.Why were you initially drawn to social epistemology?

To be honest, I was not aware that my work on the epistemic foundations of game theory, which dates back to the 80's, could be classified as social epistemology. My focus was to understand under which epistemic conditions players can reach an equilibrium, and how to discriminate among equilibria on the basis of the way players revise their beliefs about the choices of other players. I was using some tools from epistemology to understand and model players' own reasoning, so my focus was game theory, not epistemology. Of course, the *interactive epistemology* that lies at the foundation of game theory is an example of social epistemology, but neither I nor the other philosophers interested in the epistemic foundations of game theory conceived of our work in those terms. Only later, when I started working on social norms, I recognized the importance of social epistemology, in the sense that if we understand norms as supported by social expectations, we need to be very specific in defining such expectations, and how they emerge and change.

I have also been interested in the "we-intentions" literature, since it was hypothesized that group identity could explain the effects of pre-play group discussion in social dilemmas. I debated this issue for a long time with my late friend Robyn Dawes, who was convinced that pre-play communication, and the ensuing high levels of cooperation, are due to the formation of group identity through communication. Group identity is certainly important when we have an in-group/out-group situation, but there is no evidence that it has an effect when the same group is involved in a discussion of the game. The really interesting phenomenon is that players, when they can discuss the game, will often make public promises and commit to cooperate. Even in anonymous encounters, they then stick to their promises. I have suggested that this type of communication elicits social norms, and subsequent experiments substantiate this conjecture (Bicchieri 2002; Bicchieri and Lev-On 2007).

2. What are your main contributions to the field of social epistemology?

My work on the epistemic foundations of game theory, for one (Bicchieri 2007). More recently, my work on social norms and the analysis of expectations, normative and empirical, that support them (Bicchieri 2006). A norm is a social institution, but it would not exist without the web of social expectations that make it a norm. When a large enough number of people believe that a large proportion of the relevant population follows a determinate behavioral rule, and also believe that a large proportion of that population think they should follow that rule, we have a good starting point for a norm to exist. Of course, beliefs alone do not motivate. So it must also be the case that the belief holders have a preference to conform to that specific behavioral rule, but their preference is conditional on having those beliefs. Normative and empirical expectations are necessary, but not sufficient, to make a behavioral rule a norm. We share a lot of customs and conventions that are not social norms, and it is important to know the difference. It is especially important if we are interested in social change, because change often involves a change in beliefs and expectations. An operational definition of norms (in terms of expectations and conditional preferences) allows us to check whether a change in expectations causes a change in behavior, and whether empirical or normative expectations are the source of change. I have done several behavioral experiments to check just that: if we manipulate expectations, what happens? It is a very relevant question to ask if we are interested in understanding what determines pro-social behavior, and under which conditions individuals will be fair or unfair, cooperative or not. My results show quite clearly that many individuals who behave in a fair way under certain conditions revert to selfishness if we change their expectations (Bicchieri and Chavez 2010). It seems a depressing conclusion, but in fact it gives us hope that, by changing the environmental conditions, we may be able to improve social cooperation.

An important part of my experimental work has been assessing expectations independently of observation. We want to know if a norm exists for the participants, and also whether they are sensitive to it, or under what sort of conditions they will obey it. So we want to measure consensus that a norm exists and is relevant to the present situation, as well as compliance, or under which conditions a norm will be followed. We start by asking participants what their personal normative beliefs are, and then ask again what they think the majority of participants responded. If these second-order beliefs are mutually consistent, we can be pretty sure that a norm is in place. One might expect that first and second-order beliefs are also consistent, but this may not always be the case. With important pro-social norms such as reciprocity, first and second-order beliefs are usually in harmony; for example, if I ask a number of people whether they believe one should reciprocate a favor, they will usually respond that yes, one should, and if I ask them what they believe the majority responded, they will correctly say that the majority believe favors should be reciprocated. Yet there are many situations in which we may observe an inconsistency between what people think is appropriate behavior and the behavior they believe others endorse. These are what I call "belief traps".

For example, suppose the perceived norm among a group of schoolteachers is to be tough with the students. Individually, most teachers may believe that this is not the right attitude, but they fear expressing their views since what they observe is strict behavior. Telling what they really think may put them at a disadvantage among their colleagues. They may infer from observing stern behavior that the other teachers endorse severity, and wrongly conclude they are the only deviants in the group, even more reason not to vent their opinion. This phenomenon is what social psychologists call 'pluralistic ignorance', and I believe it is quite widespread. An interesting link I discovered is one between pluralistic ignorance and informational cascades (Bicchieri and Fukui 1999). In a state of pluralistic ignorance, individuals have private information about their preferences and beliefs, but can only infer other people's preferences or beliefs from observing their choices. If they assume that other people's choices truthfully reveal their preferences, beliefs, or attitudes, they may find it rational to conform to patterns of behavior they privately dislike. In other words, pluralistic ignorance is likely to generate informational cascades, i.e., it is optimal for an individual, having observed the actions of other individuals, to follow their behavior regardless of her own preferences or private information. Once an individual acts only on the information obtained from others' actions, her decision conveys no truthful information about her private information or preferences. Because the conformity of individuals in a cascade has no informational value, cascades are fragile and could be upset by the arrival of new (truthful) public information. This is how 'bad' norms may emerge and persist, but also quickly disappear.

Another area of interest has been to determine when people *choose* to get information. Is our desire to acquire new information context-dependent? If so, how? Take information that would reveal what the accepted norm is. In ambiguous situations, we might want to know what other people usually do or think appropriate. Erte Xiao and I tested subjects in a Dictator game (Xiao and Bicchieri 2012). In this type of game, it is not obvious that one should share the money or instead keep it all or, if giving some, how much to give. However, we know that, if we give participants information about what others in previous games did (or said should be done), behavior will conform to the message (Bicchieri and Xiao 2009). We discovered that 80% of dictators were unwilling to spend even a tiny amount of money to get information about what others do or approve of in an identical situation. It seems that individuals "prefer not to know" in a context that, because of its inherent ambiguity, allows for self-serving behavior. If people are not willing to incur costs to obtain norm-revealing information, whether information affects decision-making will depend on the diffusion, transparency and accessibility of the information. In cases where norm-relevant information is freely available, people's behavior will be influenced by the observation of what others do or by knowing what others expect them to do. In contrast, when norm-relevant information is less transparent and costly to obtain, there should be more variability of individual behavior and more selfish choices, as individuals will not make an effort to find out information about what other people do or believe ought to be done. These conclusions have obvious policy implications.

My interest in self-serving biases has also led me to study how people choose what to believe. Again, when situations are ambiguous, we observe a tendency to choose behaviors that benefit the individual, often at a cost to other parties (Xiao and Bicchieri 2010). Yet these choices are not obviously and blatantly selfish. Individuals tend to choose selfish behaviors that can be publicly justified as reasonable, i.e. that third parties uninvolved in the situation would find acceptable (Bicchieri and Mercier 2013). If we elicit the beliefs of the 'selfish' choosers, we see that they tend to believe that their behavior can be expected even by their 'victims', and can be justified by individuals uninvolved in the choice situation. These results are supported by the literature on motivated reasoning. Many experiments have shown that people are apt to find rationalizations for behavior they want to engage in (Valdesolo and DeSteno 2008). Yet their ability to rationalize their behavior is not unlimited: they need to find a reason for their behavior that, they think, would pass muster with the relevant audience (Kunda 1990).

3. What is the proper role of social epistemology in relation to other disciplines?

Insofar as a discipline deals with mutual knowledge and beliefs, and the social dimension of belief formation, change and knowledge in general, it deals with social epistemology.

4. What are the most important open problems in social epistemology and what are the prospects for progress?

The construction and the transmission of knowledge are social processes. Not exclusively social, but importantly so. It is thus very important to be aware of, and explore, how the social dimension of knowledge operates. I am not just referring to the work that has been done on the sociology of knowledge, and of science in particular. Or the interesting work on testimony, and its relation to power. What I find interesting and quite unexplored is the role of communication in the process of belief formation and change.

I was recently discussing with a UNICEF representative about the difficulties of changing factual beliefs in African villages where mothers believe that giving babies colostrum is dangerous, whereas giving them water is helpful. The water is often badly polluted, the children get sick and die, but no connection is made between the water and the diseases that plague the children. Explaining the connection is hard, as those people believe in magic as a source of disease and death. Thinking about factual belief change made me think about testimony, and how we learn new facts. We learn new things all the time, and only seldom from direct experience. We generally trust our sources of information, we are disposed to learn when what we read or are told comes from a credible source. So I think the problem of credibility has to be addressed in conjunction with an analysis of belief formation and revision. It is a complex problem, because credibility goes both ways. The credible source might lose credibility if it reveals information that goes against the audience's core beliefs and/or values. Hugo Mercier and I have looked at some interesting data generated by Tostan, an NGO that works with many African villages that have been involved in female genital cutting for hundreds of years (Bicchieri and Mercier, 2014). How were they convinced to change? How did their beliefs evolve? The most interesting element that emerged from this analysis was that collective discussion, taking place over at least three years, made people aware that there were contradictions between some of their core beliefs and values and other beliefs and practices they commonly endorsed. Female genital cutting was linked to ideas of family honor, purity, and stereotypical female roles. But these people also cared about the well being of their daughters, their bodily integrity, and their ultimate happiness. An extensive, guided discussion about core values and beliefs, and what they may entail, brought about a new awareness that there were contradictions between some practices and core beliefs and values. The collective, protracted discussion led to several important changes, including the abandonment of female genital cutting. We all strive for consistency, and discussing together helps to expose contradictory beliefs and negotiate belief changes.

Of course collective discussion might also have more sinister results: polarization, conformist beliefs and 'groupthink' are just some of the possible effect of collective deliberation. What we need to study are the conditions that make deliberation a genuine conduit to change.

I am a believer in the empirical dimension of philosophy. We may have a great normative theory, but if it is very distant from human's actual capabilities, it is useless. There are many issues that are of great empirical relevance to which social epistemology can give a contribution, but its contribution will depend upon trying to understand how, for example, people's beliefs change, and then giving a model of belief change that reflects how we actually reason. Future models of belief formation and change should study, among other things, what are the conditions that allow for 'good', genuine collective deliberation.

References

Bicchieri, C. and Fukui, Y. (1999). "The Great Illusion: Ignorance, Informational Cascades and the Persistence of Unpopular Norms", *Business Ethics Quarterly* 9: 127-155

Bicchieri, C. (2002). "Covenants without swords: group identity, norms, and communication in social dilemmas", *Rationality and Society* 14(2): 192-228

Bicchieri, C. (2006). *The Grammar of Society: the Nature and Dynamics of Social Norms*, Cambridge University Press

Bicchieri, C. (2007). "Game Theory: Some Personal Reflections," *Game Theory 5 Questions*, V. F. Hendricks and P. G. Hansen (eds.), Automatic Press.

Bicchieri, C. and Lev-On, A. (2007). "Computer-Mediated Communication and Cooperation in Social Dilemmas: An Experimental Analysis", *Politics, Philosophy and Economics*, vol.6: 139-168.

Bicchieri, C. and Xiao, E. (2009). "Do the right thing: but only if others do so", *Journal of Behavioral Decision Making* 22: 191-208.

Bicchieri, C. and Chavez, A. (2010). "Behaving as Expected: Public Information and Fairness Norms", *Journal of Behavioral Decision Making*, 23 (2): 161-178

Bicchieri, C. and Mercier, H. (2013). "Self-serving Biases and Public Justification in Trust games", *Synthese* 190, 5: 909-922

Bicchieri, C. and Mercier, H. (2014) "Norms and beliefs: How change occurs", Iyyun: The Jerusalem Philosophical Quarterly 63, 2014.

Reprinted in B. Edmonds (ed.) The Complexity of Social Norms. SpringerKunda, Z. (1990). "The case for motivated reasoning". *Psychological Bulletin*, *108*, 480- 498.

Valdesolo, P. and DeSteno, D. (2008). "The duality of virtue: Deconstructing the moral hypocrite". *Journal of Experimental Social Psychology* 44: 1334–1338.

Xiao, E. and Bicchieri, C. (2010). "When Equality Trumps Reciprocity", *Journal of Economic Psychology* 31 (3): 456-470.

Xiao, E. and Bicchieri, C. (2012). "Words or Deeds? Choosing what to Know about Others" *Synthese,* 187 (1): 49-63

4

Lorraine Code

Distinguished Research Professor Emerita

Department of Philosophy, York University Toronto, Canada

---

1. Why were you initially drawn to social epistemology?

In my view, the principal appeal of social epistemology is in its promise, implicit in the title itself, to close a gap between formal epistemology reliant on 'S-knows-that-p' exemplars of propositional knowledge or Gettier-style problems and their analogues, on the one hand, and the quotidian knowledge-seeking and -communicating projects of people in the real world, on the other. Attesting to a conviction that philosophy can and should contribute to human capacities to understand the world and 'our' place in it, and that knowing well is crucial to achieving that end, social epistemology seems to be well equipped to make such a contribution. It claims its title, in large measure, from the centrality it accords to knowledge-conveying exchanges between and among interlocutors, and especially to issues surrounding testimonial exchange; and it is striking for the attention many practitioners give to extended, situated examples of epistemic deliberation and negotiation. Equally noteworthy are linguistic shifts from impersonal, third-person propositional claims that "S knows that p" to the language of speakers and hearers evident, paradigmatically, in Edward Craig's *Knowledge and the State of Nature*, and Miranda Fricker's *Epistemic Injustice*,[1] where the Fricker text is innovative, also, in its attention to how power and privilege figure in knowledge exchanges, and in the *ethics* of knowing.

More fundamentally, and of a piece with these considerations, social epistemology (albeit to varying degrees) departs from the individualism of the epistemologies of the Anglo-American mainstream, to start from a recognition of how minuscule a portion of what people rightly claim to know can, or indeed could, be known by separate, self-contained 'individuals' remote from and uninfluenced by any other human being(s). The idea of the isolated, self-sufficient knower collecting, and verifying

---

[1] Edward Craig, *Knowledge and the State of Nature: An Essay in Conceptual Synthesis*, Oxford: Clarendon Press, 1990; Miranda Fricker, *Epistemic Injustice: Power and the Ethics of Knowing*, Oxford: Oxford University Press, 2007.

or falsifying, knowledge claims by her/his efforts alone is incongruous with the interdependence of human lives, even at a basic perceptual, biological and psychological level, and still more incongruous in complex knowledge-seeking projects. Social epistemology presupposes this interdependence and situatedness, to work from and with it, rather than abstracting from it to construct examples of ideal knowing. In many of its modalities it takes into account (situationally salient) differences that distinguish would-be knowers, singly or collectively, from one another and require complex negotiations if knowledge-production and circulation are to be democratically inclusive in addressing, and being accessible to, the putative knowers and the people allegedly known and addressed in state-of-the-art knowledge.[2]

While the formal S-knows-that-p rubric seemed to enable early-twentieth-century Anglo-American epistemologists to achieve certainty by transcending the vicissitudes of the world en route to determining a priori necessary and sufficient conditions for "knowledge in general", social epistemologists return to and reclaim the world, both human and other-than-human, with its inherent sociality, its incoherence and messiness, its contradictions and specificities, to engage in epistemic interactions and deliberations in which the very idea of "knowledge in general" is emptied of content. Social epistemology generates a range of issues that, for traditional epistemologists, counted merely as *hors de question*, many of which blur the dividing lines that have separated epistemological inquiry from ethical and political debate and influences. In many versions of social epistemology, ethical-political questions - such putatively extra-epistemological issues as trust, power, credibility, advocacy, negotiation, and epistemic community - enter the discourse, and not to the detriment of responsibly objective inquiry. Giving and receiving testimony commonly, if tacitly, involves many of these issues. The larger point, then, is that social epistemology engages with knowledge-making practices as fully as it addresses and analyses (perhaps interim) conclusions. Implicit in this claim is a blurring, also, of the line that has traditionally separated the contexts of discovery and justification from one another: a blurring that is evident in construing these contexts as reciprocally constitutive.

Although some traditional *ethical* theories have seemed to offer action-guiding principles and ideals relevant to the specificities of human lives, Anglo-American epistemology before social epistemology has rarely provided analogous knowledge-guiding principles, pertinent to the variability of quotidian knowledge-producing practices. This con-

---

[2] See, for example, the essays in Heidi Grasswick, ed., *Feminist Epistemology and Philosophy of Science: Power in Knowledge*. Dordrecht: Springer, 2012.

trast is, admittedly, exaggerated with respect to ethical theory as such, so to speak, since feminist, non-white, and other post-colonial ethical theorists have exposed and critiqued a formal remoteness from diverse, messy human lives and from particular, real-world moral dilemmas that is characteristic of classical utilitarian, deontological, and Rawlsian theories.[3] But some connections with actions and concrete situations are at least implicit – if often in attenuated fashion – in exemplary moral conundrums, whereas formality remains the preferred mode of much Anglo-American twentieth-century and early twenty-first-century epistemology before, or apart from, social epistemology.

A significant aspect of social epistemology's departure from formality is in its (in general) minimal concentration on logical possibility, while taking seriously the extent to which practical possibilities integral to situations, circumstances, and uneven distributions of power and privilege, constrain and/or enable knowledge projects in achieving their ends. Logical possibility diminishes in relevance once situational, material obstacles and/or enhancements are taken seriously, and the idea that knowers are always somewhere, and limited or enabled accordingly, claims a central place on the epistemic terrain. Thus social epistemology often requires a certain attention to particularity, which has to be achieved without embarking on a potentially dangerous descent into 'particularism'. The challenge of fulfilling such a requirement is as productive as it is caution-inducing.

2. What are your main contributions to the field of social epistemology?

Epistemic Responsibility (1987)[4] is my earliest and still one of my main contributions to social epistemology, even though I did not represent it thus at the time of writing, principally because the language of social epistemology was not then current. The book has until quite recently been something of a sleeper, but now, in the second decade of the twenty-first century, its conceptual apparatus is increasingly invoked in epistemic deliberations, particularly as these relate to such urgent and contentious issues in the social-political world, as matters of social-epistemic justice, ecological/climate related questions, and issues of knowing people, institutions, and phenomena across multiple modalities of diversity. It is now cited as one of the earliest works in twentieth-century virtue epistemology, and is frequently invoked in science and

---

[3] Pertinent here is Claudia Card, *The Unnatural Lottery: Character and Moral Luck*. Philadelphia: Temple University Press, 1996.

[4] Lorraine Code, *Epistemic Responsibility*. Hanover, NH: University Press of New England, 1987.

technology studies. Later, and equally significant, are my contributions to feminist and post-colonial epistemology in *What Can She Know?* (1991) and *Rhetorical Spaces* (1995)[5]; and my analyses of testimony as a central component of knowledge production and circulation, depicted as a communicative social inquiry throughout my published work, and especially in my book *Ecological Thinking: The Politics of Epistemic Location* (2006).[6]

In all of these works, starting with *Epistemic Responsibility*, I maintain that knowing/knowledge are not just social practices but are ethically and politically implicated in human lives and indeed carry and/or foster social values and projects, if variously across situations and populations. Significant to such inquiries then is a basic acknowledgement that differences in social-cultural positioning, especially again with respect to power and privilege, play a constitutive part in determining whose knowledge claims merit a hearing and are to be taken seriously, whose testimony will claim uptake and achieve epistemic warrant, how trustworthiness and credibility are to be distributed across the social order. Hence I have maintained that the question "Whose knowledge are we talking about?" is often central to evaluating putative contributions to public knowledge. Such an acknowledgement is epistemologically fraught within a tradition that has sought to separate knowledge from power and from any facile assumption that 'might makes right'. Yet maintaining its significance amounts neither to granting veto or overriding assent to the powerful, nor to denying speaking positions to or routinely disbelieving the less powerful: it can open rhetorical spaces that are more democratic than those that are tacitly presupposed in the putative neutrality of white mainstream patriarchal, racist, classist, homophobic, and other social structures where epistemic marginalization can, overtly or covertly, be enacted and needs to be exposed and countered if spaces for democratic epistemic practice are to be kept open.

These latter thoughts are continuous with the significance I maintain for "taking subjectivity into account", in an essay by that title, which also figures centrally among my contributions to social epistemology.[7] While the very idea announced in the title may seem to recommend subjectivism in the most pernicious of senses, such is not the intention of the analysis. In one sense, taking subjectivity into account simply or not so simply entails becoming aware of who specifically (singular

5   Lorraine Code, *What Can She Know? Feminist Theory and the Construction of Knowledge*. Ithaca, NY: Cornell University Press, 1991; and *Rhetorical Spaces: Essays on (Gendered) Locations*. New York: Routledge, 1995.

6   Lorraine Code, *Ecological Thinking: The Politics of Epistemic Location*. New York: Oxford University Press, 2006.

7   Lorraine Code, "Taking Subjectivity into Account". In Code, 1995.

or plural), as contrasted with who in general, has traditionally occupied the S place in S-knows-that-p knowledge claims. Although in the positivist-empiricist tradition the occupant is presumed to be a mere place-holder, infinitely replicable in standard propositional formulations, and although such propositions tend to be constructed so that the specificities of S's identity will be irrelevant to the formal structure of the argument, a few simple substitutions have by now clearly demonstrated that the default occupant of the S-place has been male, presumptively white, and materially comfortable, with 'normal' perceptual and other capacities, and unbiased – almost a human *tabula rasa* – in his epistemic activities. Unwittingly, one must assume, such presuppositions restrict the viable population of epistemic subjects in ways that can be, and frequently are, unjust. By implication, they likewise limit the range of examples that can form the stuff of epistemic deliberation. If social epistemology is not to be restricted before the fact to an implausibly narrow range of potential knowers endeavouring to know and understand a narrow sampling of the complexities of the physical, natural, social, human and other-than-human world, then such tacit limitations have to be uncovered, made explicit, and figured in to evaluations and critiques of knowledge production.

Taking subjectivity into account entails working with and acknowledging the integral, indeed the cognitively constitutive aspects of human interdependence, and of the specificities of embodiment and affect, of situation and circumstance, in producing subjectivities with their multiple ways of being in, and knowing the world. These aspects make of social epistemology a more interpretive and dialogical project than its post-positivist proximity to a formal version of scientific inquiry had put in place as a desideratum for epistemology as such, so to speak. But these same aspects enhance its explanatory potential for engagement with the complex issues that comprise human epistemic relationships with and in the social, political, material world. They also, it must be ventured, point toward deep-seated ontological presuppositions about knowers and knowing that are by no means self-evidently universal or ubiquitously warranted. Taking subjectivity into account in its genealogical implications reveals the contingency of such presuppositions: it requires epistemologists to reexamine the foundational assumptions about subjectivity and agency that have generated and sustained the epistemologies of mastery and control that have latterly come to be the focus of feminist and other post-colonial critique.[8] It would be less than fitting to presuppose that an epistemically responsible response to

---

[8]   See Val Plumwood, *Feminism and the Mastery of Nature*. London: Routledge, 1993, which is a pivotal text for my discussion in *Ecological Thinking*.

the question "Whose knowledge are we talking about?" could, in these post-colonial times, be framed as "everyone's", where "everyone" is homogeneously construed. Social epistemology well conceived needs to work sensitively toward recognizing the epistemological effects of differences from an unarticulated human sameness. Such a claim is central, for example, to Charles Mills's exposure, in *The Racial Contract*[9] of a pervasive epistemology of ignorance that prevents white people from knowing the world that they themselves have made: a work which is emblematic for more wide-spread recognitions of how much has to be presumed and ignored in mainstream social-scientific and everyday assumptions about the ease of knowing across social-political-cultural differences. Hence just as social epistemologists are engaged in investigating the conditions that make knowledge possible, so an inquiry into the conditions that create and sustain ignorance has come to be a compelling and productive area of investigation in social epistemology.[10]

3. What is the proper role of social epistemology in relation to other disciplines?

Some philosophers might think of social epistemology as a sort of overseer with no subject matter of its own, but committed to adjudicating knowledge claims in diverse social settings and subject matters, made by diverse epistemic subjects; but such a conception would improbably restrict the range of inquiry that takes place under the "social epistemology" umbrella. While the varieties of inquiry I am including under the heading "social epistemology" may, in engaging with specific subject matters and institutions "down on the ground", so to speak, sacrifice the clarity, purity, and universal pertinence claimed for mainstream analytic epistemology, social epistemology does not, whether by definition or in practice, eschew the need to establish epistemic warrant and to engage in rigorous evaluation processes. Such processes will often be collaborative/deliberative, disputational and experimental, but they need not for that reason yield less clear and valid conclusions than more individualistic practices are reputed to deliver. They often consist in situated assessments of the subject matters and methods of inquiry internal to such disciplinary inquiries as the physical-natural and social sciences; and engage in analyses of the putative knowledge of complex, multifaceted modalities of human lives, experiences, and institutions. They address questions about how to enlist and evaluate the diverse

---

[9]   Charles Mills, *The Racial Contract*. Ithaca: Cornell University Press, 1998. See also George Yancy, ed., *The Center Must Not Hold: White Women Philosophers on the Whiteness of Philosophy*. Lanham, MD: Lexington Books, 2010.

[10]   Of interest in this regard is Shannon Sullivan and Nancy Tuana, eds., *Race and Epistemologies of Ignorance*. Albany: State University of New York Press, 2007.

forms of expertise and authority that shape inquiry in general, or in specific disciplines and subject matters. In such interventions, social epistemology plays a constructive and/or critical part in working internally, and often genealogically, with epistemic practices, exposing and evaluating patterns of inclusion and exclusion that feed into theory choice and choices that determine matters of investigation. In so doing it, examines and critiques the power and privilege relations within particular inquiries, institutions, and larger discipline, with the epistemic and social-structural injustices they often foster.[11]

Exemplary in this regard are some of the investigations detailed and analyzed in the essays in Figueroa and Harding's collection *Science and Other Cultures*[12] which I am reading as illustrative of social epistemology in action. For example, Hugh Lacey in "Seeds and their Sociocultural Nexus" compellingly suggests that "what seeds… and the plants that grow from them *are* is partly a function of the sociocultural nexus (SCN) of which they are constituents" (91, my italics), arguing that the value of seeds does not "transcend their specific nexus" and asking then how seeds, plants, crops are to be "scientifically investigated", and how the ensuing knowledge is to be evaluated. I take these questions, with their emphasis on social-cultural values, to emanate from explicitly situated social practices and from a careful recognition of social-epistemological diversity that has to be acknowledged and accommodated within an inquiry, without sliding into a mute form of relativism. Thus, in a different vein, Robert Crease, in "Fallout",[13] examines a situation of western intervention in a non-western culture which, in consequence of "unfamiliarity with the culture and the environment" (106), ended up causing harm to the very people the intervention was designed to assist. Epistemologically, in this as in numerous analogous examples, the clear implication is that it is often a mistake to assume before the fact that knowledge will "travel" intact from one social-cultural situation to another, for the errors consequent upon such assumptions can have dire material effects. Indeed, and more strongly, the default assumption has to shift from an uncontested belief in human and situational sameness to an expectation that knowledge very likely will not travel intact across

---

[11] Outstanding in this regard is Alison Wylie, "What Knowers Know Well: Women, Work and the Academy". In Heidi Grasswick, ed., *Feminist Epistemology and Philosophy of Science: Power in Knowledge*. Dordrecht: Springer, 2012.

[12] Robert Figueroa and Sandra Harding, eds., *Science and Other Cultures: Issues in Philosophies of Science and Technology*. New York: Routledge, 2003.

[13] Hugh Lacey, "Seeds and their Sociocultural Nexus" and Robert P. Crease, "Fallout: Issues in the Study, Treatment, and Reparations of Exposed Marshall Islanders", both in Figueroa and Harding, 2003.

social-political-demographic differences without the risk of enacting a range of epistemic harms. Responsible epistemic conduct has to incorporate a sensitivity to the minutiae of differences which amounts, in effect, to an elaborated awareness of the real, material dangers of hasty generalization.

Under the "social epistemology" label, then, can be included investigations that seek to discern the epistemic warrant and effectiveness of evidence based medicine (EBM), for example, by contrast with or in comparison to narrative-based, interpretive analyses and other less "scientistic", less formal diagnostic procedures. Qualitative inquiry in the social sciences, too, enlists elements of what has come to be called social epistemology. Many of these areas of investigation are contiguous, variously, with work in "Science, technology and society (STS)" where some of the theoretical tenets, commitments, and investigative approaches of social epistemologists are enlisted in conducting studies of the influences of social, political, and cultural values in shaping the agendas and methods of scientific research and technological innovation, and examining the impacts of these projects and innovations for society, politics and culture.[14] Social epistemology is a significant participant in these areas of investigation, especially in its capacity to contribute critically and constructively to the knowledge that informs social activism. STS studies, where the philosophical influence of Bruno Latour[15] among others is of major significance, are noteworthy for their widespread influence in shaping investigations of knowledge, science, and society as much in European as in Anglo-American philosophy. As might be expected, the "social constructivist" thesis Latour and his colleagues apparently endorse has not garnered unqualified approval from social epistemologists more generally, especially given its apparent implication that the very entities scientists study, thus not just their representations, are socially constructed. Such a thesis seems to place their inquiry, improbably, well beyond the reach of verification or falsification, and to pose residual questions about its very meaningfulness. Hence the value of this line of inquiry for social epistemology remains an open but intriguingly provocative, and increasingly productive question.

---

[14] Thomas Kuhn, *The structure of scientific revolutions* (Chicago: University of Chicago Press, 1962) is often cited as a foundational text. See also K. Brad Wray, *Kuhn's Evolutionary Social Epistemology*, Cambridge University Press, 2011.

[15] Landmark texts are Bruno Latour, *Science in action: How to follow scientists and engineers through society.* Cambridge, MA: Harvard University Press: 1987; and Bruno Latour and Steve Woolgar, *Laboratory Life: The Construction of Scientific Facts.* Princeton, NJ: Princeton University Press. (1986 (1979)).

4. What have been the most significant advances in social epistemology?

Among the most significant advances in social epistemology since the beginning of the twenty-first century, as I have noted, is its departure, in many of its central texts, from the white-centered, western-centered, andro-centered analyses of knowledge-producing and -evaluating practices with their assumptions about human sameness, which have been one of its principal if not exclusive areas of critical focus. This shift (so far admittedly partial), together with the recommendation to take subjectivity into account, may be troubling to traditional epistemologists bent on determining necessary and sufficient conditions for the achievement of knowledge in general, for such attention to epistemic diversity, again, will seem to condone and even to propose a descent into a pernicious form of relativism for which all claims to know are up for grabs and no overarching criteria for determining truth or falsity can prevail. Such a worry can be dispelled in at least two ways: first, it is readily apparent from examining social epistemology at work, so to speak, that the aim is not to abandon verification or justificatory standards for the diverse knowledge claims and knowledge-producing practices social epistemologists are prepared to take seriously. The worry is generated in part by an adherence to a stark and indeed implausible set of dichotomies according to which any degree of relativity is opposed to and thus abandons realism, rationality, and objectivity: a dichotomy analyzed as the rational/social dichotomy by Helen Longino, in *The Fate of Knowledge*[16] and shown to be neither truth-denying nor so stark as has commonly been assumed. Second, such a worry presupposes and emanates from an epistemology of interchangeable individuals where knowers are isolated units on an indifferent landscape and where no epistemic interaction can or should contribute to the production and evaluation of knowledge claims. Thus for example, while certain human commonalities can responsibly be presupposed in evaluations, say, of the disease reporting and diagnosing practices of some non-Western populations, interactive practices of working to discern possibilities of finding a common epistemological ground from which to move toward treatment attests to the effects of a social epistemology enlisted in practice, to achieve a solution that is both scientifically/medically effective and just, yet dismissive neither of traditional wisdom nor of modern western medical science and pharmacology.[17] In such mutually respect-

---

[16] Helen Longino, *The Fate of Knowledge*: Princeton, NJ: Princeton University Press, 2004.

[17] See for example Lorraine Code, "Advocacy, Negotiation and the Politics of Unknowing". *The Southern Journal of Philosophy*, XLVI (2008) Supp. "Global

ful critical dialogue across systems of knowledge, relative differences are taken very seriously, but relativ*ism* in a pernicious sense is not the outcome.

5. What are the most important open problems in social epistemology and what are the prospects for progress?

One of the most compelling problems social epistemologists face is that of legitimizing their inquiries within or in relation to the received conception of epistemology as such, where inquiry centres upon issues of publicly available unambiguous evidence, adjudication, and universally applicable criteria of verification and falsification. A conviction prevails in the Anglo-American mainstream that any epistemology worthy of the name will have a commitment to achieving truth and countering skepticism, and will present clear, univocal and realizable directives for so doing. Social epistemology, especially in those (=most) of its branches which adhere to a significant degree of pluralism both of practitioners and of explanation, may seem to have defaulted on this basic, definitive commitment. On this issue, social epistemologists will be obliged, then, to give credible accounts of their practice and to demonstrate the trustworthiness of their findings. Even those who discount the possibility of attaining absolute truth will be called upon to indicate what they are urging in its place that will allow their pursuits to count as appropriately epistemological, if in a renewed, reconstructed sense.

In *Ecological Thinking*, where I represent Rachel Carson as just such a thinker, and her practices of inquiry as socially based especially in their respect for 'everyday' testimony, I commend her epistemic humility in part for what Samantha Frost, in a different context, aptly calls "an acknowledgement of the impossibility of full and definitive knowledge".[18] Something of the sort becomes a more widespread directive in many social epistemological projects, I am suggesting, without reducing to a facile suggestion – again – that "anything goes", but amounting rather to a recognition that the interim but often solid conclusions of inductive inference may well have to be the end points of certain complex processes of inquiry, with definitive, complete knowledge either a rare achievement, or an unattainable goal. To see this issue as a problem for social epistemology is not to suggest that a sure and irrefutable route to definitive knowledge has to be determined if social epistemology is to earn the "epistemology" part of its title; but rather to suggest that a way of making peace with carefully achieved

Feminist Ethics and Politics", 32- 51.

[18] Samantha Frost, "The Implications of the New Materialisms for Feminist Epistemology". In Grasswick, ed., 2012.

knowledge, good of its kind, open to critical scrutiny but mixed with a
certain indeterminacy may be what social epistemologists have to endorse as their goal, while demonstrating to the philosophical profession
or a doubting public that their practice is worthy, responsible, truth-
respecting, and realistic.

Internal to social epistemological projects themselves, when knowledge is represented as communal and/or 'commonable' (to borrow
Michael Welbourne's term[19]), is the question of how to assign responsibility and where to direct criticism for items of knowledge that are
represented as everyone's and no one's. This is a large issue: to whom
can the authorship of climate change skepticism be attributed, or of the
unexpected consequences of DDT in attempts to eradicate malaria? If,
as Lynn Hankinson Nelson argues, it is communities who construct and
communicate knowledge and who determine standards of evidence,
then communities must be the primary knowers (256).[20] Nelson's point
is that to understand why a theory or a set of knowledge claims gains
assent at a certain time and place, requires investigating the relevant
community as contrasted with the beliefs and knowledge of "individual" knowers. Yet on such a view it is difficult to see how the question "Whose knowledge are we talking about?" can be answered well
enough to indicate who can claim credit, or who should be criticized,
for its success or failures in furthering epistemic and practical ends.
The very idea of communal or commonable knowledge is at once persuasive and puzzling, especially in investigating how it can fit within
or dislodge assumptions of knowledge as an individual achievement
and possession. That such assumptions have outworn their usefulness
is one of the lessons social epistemology seems to suggest, but it is
unclear how to respond to the questions that remain open. Implicated
here again is the outstanding question about power differentials and the
level or otherwise playing field on which knowledge claims are made
and uptake is to be expected. Here, Wittgenstein's observation "Knowledge is in the end based on acknowledgement"[21], to which I have ap-
pealed through much of my work, has some claim to emblematic status
in catching the promise and the problems of social epistemology, so
long as it is read as an appeal to the social character of knowing, yet not
as arguing for a consensus theory of truth.

---

[19] Michael Welbourne, *Knowledge*. Montreal: McGill-Queen's University Press,
2001.

[20] Lynn Hankinson Nelson, *Who Knows: From Quine to a Feminist Empiricism*.
Philadelphia: Temple University Press. 1990.

[21] Ludwig Wittgenstein, *On Certainty*. Eds., G.E.M. Anscombe and G. H. von
Wright; Trans. Denis Paul and G.E.M. Anscombe. Oxford: Basil Blackwell, 1968,
§378.

5

Hans van Ditmarsch

Senior Researcher

LORIA - CNRS/University of Lorraine, France & IMSc (Institute of Mathematical Sciences), Chennai, India

---

1. Why were you initially drawn to social epistemology?

I find it difficult to answer this question as different from why I was initially drawn to epistemic logic. I think we can say that a strong focus of social epistemology is the analysis of group beliefs, group knowledge — and their justification indeed, but I always found that hard to tackle, even in more technical settings as Artemov's justified common knowledge. So let me answer what draws me to the analysis of group notions of belief.

Well, I have always been very interested in the original sources of such matters. For common knowledge and common belief, Lewis' Convention [7] is often quoted but that are various other 1960s and 1970s sources [6, 9]. John McCarthy's ideas on common knowledge relate it to fixed points. In a small piece of writing that at the stage he did not even consider to be of enough importance to publish — it was only later included in an overview of previously unpublished notes [9] — McCarthy formalizes two logical puzzles, one called the 'Wise Men' puzzle (this is also known as 'Muddy Children'), and another puzzle about numbers, called the 'Sum and Product'-riddle. In the course of solving those riddles, using first-order logical terminology, he almost off-handedly introduces the reflexive transitive closure of accessibility relations. Now an interesting aspect is that he does so with an axiomatization in first-order logic and a corresponding first-order logic theorem prover (FOL, by Weyhrauch, see e.g. [13]), and not with modal operators. Citing McCarthy:

> The axiomatization has the following features. It is entirely in first order logic rather than in modal logic. The Kripke accessibility relation is axiomatized. No knowledge operator or function is used.

> We hope to present a second axiomatization using
> a knowledge function, but we haven't yet decided
> how to handle time and learning in such an axio-
> matization.[9]

Famous last words! Another interesting aspect is that he does so not just for individual agents, but indeed for groups of agents, thus computing reflexive transitive closures as used to interpret common knowledge and common belief operators. These are needed to process what agents commonly learn from announcements made in those riddles.

But the literature does not stop to surprise me. I recently discovered that the opening pages of Littlewood's 'A Mathematician's Miscellany' [8] contain a description and solution of the muddy children problem, the one bothering epistemic logicians for a long time because of its common knowledge aspects. And this is from the 1950s.

Recent studies as Michael Chwe's [3] keep this topic in the awareness of the public eye and of the researchers, I admire greatly Chwe's successful attempt to 'sell' a topic so clearly relevant for social epistemology.

2. What are your main contributions to the field of social epistemology?

The distinction between, on the one hand, knowledge and belief as modal operators needed to express uncertainty between a number of well-described alternatives and, on the other hand, awareness and unawareness as operators (not necessarily modal) needed to express incomplete information has been capturing my attention for a number of years and results are beginning to trickle in. What I find appealing about modelling combinations of knowledge and awareness in relation to knowledge and awareness dynamics is its relevance for bounded rationality (namely as bounded resources / restricted memory) and how to put the effort for structuring models into the dynamics, on the go, as proper in conversational analysis. This is very different from the usual way of constructing enormous initial models with lots of dazzling detail that seems to make epistemic logic a highly unsuitable tool for the analysis of social interaction. With a toolbox for unawareness, this can all become different. You start with nothing. Gradually, you increase the complexity of your models. Let us give an example.

Vincent is going to a conference. He wakes up in the morning. His mind is empty. He is utterly unaware of his surroundings and even of himself. This situation is best characterized as:

•

In words: a singleton domain Kripke model for an empty set of agents and an empty set of propositional variables, and therefore with an empty accessibility relation, and no valuation of atoms. Still, some formulas are true in this state: $\top$ (for 'true'), $\neg\bot$ ('not false'), $\top \vee \neg\bot$, and so on.

A sprinkling of self-awareness starts to invade Vincent's mind. He is able to reflect on his judgements again, yet another day! At this stage, the only things he is able to avoid are contradictions, but there are no issues to reason about yet. This situation can be visualized as:

Vincent is the agent a, who has full access to the singleton domain. Already, there is lots more to reason about. The following formulas are true in this state: $K_a\top$ ('Vincent knows true'), $K_a\neg K_a\bot$, $\top\vee K_a K_a\neg\bot$, and so on. Vincent knows that he can avoid contradictions, and that he does not know falsehoods, etc. With self-awareness, higher-order cognition has arrived!

Being aware of himself, and still rubbing stardust from his sleepy eyes, Vincent realizes what is lacking: coffee. He starts to wonder if coffee would already be served in the restaurant below. It is still fairly early. Vincent has reached the stage that he can reason about something, namely an actual proposition p (coffee is served) that he is uncertain about. This situation can be visualized as:

$$a \;\; \overset{\curvearrowright}{\underset{\curvearrowleft}{\neg p}} \leftarrow a \rightarrow p \;\; \overset{\curvearrowright}{\underset{}{}} a$$

The things that are now true are beginning to look more and more like modal logic: $Ka(\neg K_a p \wedge \neg K_a\neg p)$ (Vincent knows that he does not know whether coffee is served), $\neg K_a p$ (Vincent does not know that coffee is served), etc. In fact, no coffee is served. The actual state in the figure, where p is false, is therefore underlined.

Now, while on his way to the lower floor, where the restaurant is located, someone in the elevator mentions that you can't have both coffee and beer for breakfast. This makes Vincent aware that beer is an issue. (Assuming that, before that, he was not indeed! I do not know him that well.) After this, Vincent does not know whether coffee is served and also does not know whether beer is served. But he knows that coffee and beer are not both served. We now get to the following situation. Unfortunately, Vincent has still not found out that the breakfast area is closed. So actually (underlined), there is no coffee and no beer.

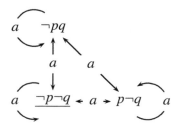

It has now become true that $K_a \neg(p \wedge q)$, and so on.

Starting with mere uncertainty about coffee, and forgetting the beer complications right above: there is yet another possible scenario, one wherein Duncan also enters the picture. Vincent recalls (i.e., he *becomes aware*) that Duncan arrived a day earlier at the conference. Duncan would certainly know if the restaurant is open or closed. And Vincent assumes he and Duncan would have been informed if the restaurant had been open, and that Duncan may have thought Vincent had already found out in another way if it had been closed. The resulting picture then becomes:

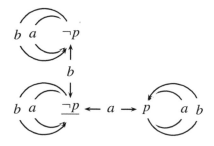

From now on, the full range of multi-agent epistemic logic is at our (and Vincent's, and Duncan's) disposition. In the underlined state it is true that Duncan does not know whether Vincent knows p: $\neg K_b(K_a p \vee K_a \neg p)$, that Vincent does not consider it possible that Duncan knows that p: $\neg\neg K_a \neg K_b p$, and so on.

One way to model this in a logic is, given a parameter set of propositional variables, to distinguish 'aware' propositional variables from 'unaware' propositional variables. This semantic setup was introduced in [4]. 'Becoming aware' in that setting is then shifting a variable from the unaware set to the aware set. The increased complexity of the models while an agent becomes aware is that we reason about equivalence classes of such models: if you ignore the value of q in the three-pointed model, the two-pointed model wherein Vincent is uncertain about coffee and the three-pointed model involving uncertainty about coffee and about beer are the same in the sense of bisimilar [2]. This modelling of awareness then becomes an exercise in bisimulation quantification.

And, similarly, this whole story holds for agent variables. Now what I really like about this, is that this logic therefore has a need for an infinite number of agents! Because at any moment, when modelling a conversation between several persons, yet someone else can enter the room and join in. So, any finite number would be insufficient to describe all possible ways of becoming aware and unaware, and ensuing belief changes. Do you know of any logic that really needs an infinite number of agents?

My work on such matters, in collaboration with others such as Tim French, Fernando Velazquez, and, more recently, Yi Wang, has been described in [10, 11].

3. What is the proper role of social epistemology in relation to other disciplines?

I have no idea. Provide insight? Make progress?

4. What have been the most significant advances in social epistemology?

All I think of involves group beliefs and the complications involving belief change. So, I would think of Arrow's theorem in social choice theory: when voters have at least three alternatives (candidates), no rank order voting system can convert the preferences of individuals into a collective preference (while also meeting certain criteria, mainly non-dictatorship) [1]. I would certainly also list the general area of pluralistic ignorance, and fascinating phenomena like information cascades — wouldn't prime minister Rajoy of Spain like to know more about irrational herd movements of bankers in the crazy economic times of the year 2012.

5. What are the most important open problems in social epistemology and what are the prospects for progress?

Thinking about that, I came up with a list, and then thought I'd better check that with my answer to 'What are the most important open problems' in the five questions volume on epistemic logic. And they were the same! Not good. So, what I did is transfer one of those problems to 'What are my main contributions', in that way suggesting scientific progress, and come up with (at least) another important open problem here: modeling uncertainty in voters.

Take the example of plurality voting. Consider two voters 1, 2, four candidates a, b, c, d, and three profiles as below. A profile lists for each voter, its preference on the set of candi- dates. For example, in the table on the left we have that voter 1 prefers a over c over b over d and that voter 2 prefers d over c over b over a. Now voter 1 is uncertain about the voting preference of voter 2 and voter 2 is uncertain about the voting preference of voter 1. This uncertainty is modelled, as usual in a modal epistemic logic, as indistinguishability, in this case: between profiles. Profile names that are indistinguishable for a voter i are linked with an i-labelled edge. The partition for 1 on the domain is therefore {{Left, Middle}, {Right}}, and the partition for 2 on the domain is {{Left}, {Middle, Right}}.

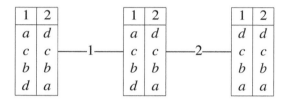

Consider a plurality vote with a tie-breaking rule $b \succ a \succ c \succ d$. (I.e., if b and a get the same number of votes, b wins. Etc.) If there had been no uncertainty, then in the profile of Middle (and Left), if 1 votes for her preference a and 2 votes for his preference d, then the tie prefers a, 2's least preferred candidate. If instead 2 votes c, a will still win. But if 2 votes b, b wins. We can observe that (a, b) and (b, b) are equilibria pairs of votes, and that for 1 voting a is dominant. Also, if there had been no uncertainty, then in the profile of Right the pair (d, d) is the dominant equilibrium.

This situation changes when we take the uncertainty of the voters into account. We need to adjust the definition of equilibrium to take the uncertainty into account. This can be called 'conditional equilibrium', its meaning might be clear from this mere example. On the condition that voters are risk averse there are two equilibria that we can associate with this model, the conditions for the strategies below should be seen as 'execution preconditions' that are only satisfied in some but not all profiles of the model (e.g., 1 prefers a is only satisfied in Left and Middle):

- (if 1 prefers *a* then 1 votes *a* and if 1 prefers *d* then 1 votes *d*, 2 votes *b*),

- (if 1 prefers *a* then 1 votes *b* and if 1 prefers *d* then 1 votes *d*, 2 votes *b*).

Unfortunately for voter 2, if the actual profile is such that *d* is his equilibrium vote, he will still not be inclined to cast that vote because he considers it possible that the profile is one wherein 1 prefers *a*, such that, if 2 votes *d* and 1 votes *a, a* gets elected, voter 2's least preferred candidate. As 2 is risk averse his (known) equilibrium vote is therefore *b*.

If both voters prefer d the case, voter 1 has an incentive to make her voting preference known to 2, and even to declare her vote prior to 2. And this can also be modelled in epistemic logic, namely in dynamic epistemic logic, with announcements. For more information, see [12].

Now here comes, I think, the interesting part. The example demonstrates that under uncertainty about others' beliefs, agents may deviate from their best interests and then reach suboptimal outcomes. On the right, both agents/voters want *d* to be elected but given the uncertainty this will still not happen. Now doesn't this remind us of pluralistic ignorance? People who change their behaviour given the uncertainty about others even though the others have similar beliefs? And maybe also of information cascades, discount- ing the irrational justification of behavioural change in that case? Yes, I'd say! So, my hope would be that, building on recent progress in that direction like Jens Ulrik Hansen's PhD thesis [5], the tools and techniques of modal logic can be useful to implement new directions in social epistemology.

Bibliography

[1] K.J. Arrow. A difficulty in the concept of social welfare. Journal of Political Economy, 58(4):328346, 1950.

[2] P. Blackburn, M. de Rijke, and Y. Venema. Modal Logic. Cambridge University Press, Cambridge, 2001. Cambridge Tracts in Theoretical Computer Science 53.

[3] M.S.-Y. Chwe. Rational Ritual. Princeton University Press, Princeton, NJ, USA, 2001.

[4] R. Fagin and J.Y. Halpern. Belief, awareness, and limited reasoning. Artificial Intel- ligence, 34(1):39–76, 1988.

[5] J.U. Hansen. A logic toolbox for modeling knowledge and information in multi-agent systems and social epistemology. PhD thesis, Roskilde University, 2011.

[6] J. Heal. Common knowledge. The Philosophical Quarterly, 28(111):116–131, 1978.

[7] D.K. Lewis. Convention, a Philosophical Study. Harvard University Press, Cambridge (MA), 1969.

[8] J.E. Littlewood. A Mathematician's Miscellany. Methuen and company, 1953.

[9] J. McCarthy. Formalization of two puzzles involving knowledge. In V. Lifschitz, editor, Formalizing Common Sense : Papers by John McCarthy, Ablex Series in Artificial Intelligence. Ablex Publishing Corporation, Norwood, N.J., 1990. original manuscript dated 1978–1981.

[10] H. van Ditmarsch and T. French. Becoming aware of propositional variables. In M. Banerjee and A. Seth, editors, Logic and Its Applications - 4th Indian Conference, ICLA 2011. Proceedings, pages 204–218. Springer, 2011. LNCS 6521.

[11] H. van Ditmarsch, T. French, and F. Velazquez-Quesada. Action models for knowledge and awareness. Proceedings of AAMAS Valencia, 2012.

[12] H. van Ditmarsch, J. Lang, and A. Saffidine. Strategic voting and the logic of knowledge.
Proceedings of 14th TARK, Chennai, 10 pages, 2013 (poster),
http://arxiv.org/abs/1310.6436 Also:
Proceedings of 11th AAMAS, Valencia, pages 1247 – 1248, 2012 (poster).

[13] R. W. Weyhrauch. Prolegomena to a theory of formal reasoning. Artificial Intelligence, 13:133–170, 1980.

6

Miranda Fricker

Professor of Philosophy
University of Sheffield

---

1. Why were you initially drawn to social epistemology?

My answer to this question is a story, which begins when I was a student. I was instinctively drawn to what are now recognised as questions in social epistemology. What drew me in was an inchoate and troubled interest in the idea that there were all sorts of connections between social identity, power, and epistemic authority that were stubbornly difficult to articulate in the recognized idiom of Anglo-American philosophy. A sense that there was nonetheless surely something worth saying that might actually be said in this foreign territory was what led me into any kind of research in philosophy.

As an MA student—on an interdisciplinary Women's Studies MA—I read some feminist philosophy. It was a revelation. These theorists were asking what struck me then, as now, to be entirely natural and compelling philosophical questions, yet questions I had never heard posed elsewhere. Questions such as, How does social power influence how we perceive and deal with each other as knowers and reasoners? How do gender, race and class affect epistemic authority? These and related questions were not of course expressed quite like that in those days. They were expressed rather in the terms proper to the feminist theory of the time, most of which drew valiantly on the only discourses in town that made questions of power seem remotely relevant to matters epistemic. These were principally Marxism (especially Lakatos who emphasised the idea of an epistemically privileged 'standpoint' of the proletariat), postmodernism (and the 'Continental' philosophers that gave that Zeitgeist its philosophical articulation—Foucault, Deleuze, Derrida), and also psychoanalysis (especially Lacan, and the French feminist theorists who championed what came to be thought of as 'difference feminism', notably Irigaray and Kristeva). As a consequence, the sorts of questions that were floating around were: Is there a standpoint of women as there is a standpoint of the proletariat? Does this standpoint enjoy any kind of epistemic privilege? What is situated knowledge? Is

reason a form of social power? Is the very idea of objectivity a subli-
mated assertion of power? Is reason masculine? Is language phallocen-
tric? and so on and so forth.

I found myself in complete disagreement with answers to any of these
questions that made one or other pseudo-radical move (as I saw it) that
reduced reason to social power, or handed over human rational or linguistic capacities to an exclusively masculine psycho-sexual make-up.
How absurd. Reason was mine, reason was ours—with feminists like
these, I wondered, who needs sexists? All this was a useful spur. I was,
however, in fascinated sympathy with the politicising spirit of these
questions—in sympathy with the thought that at least some of them
were questions worth asking, and that perhaps all of them could be
asked in a form that rendered them deeply interesting. And some feminist philosophers were posing the questions in that way, and developing
their theoretical stances with marvellous lucidity and creativity. First,
the question about reason and masculinity, for instance, makes perfect
sense so long as we are talking about constructions or imaginings of
reason—the history of philosophy, and the imaginary of philosophy, as
these might be found to reflect wider social attitudes to gender. Further,
the various related attempts to disrupt the over-confident, narrowly ra-
tionalistic sensibility so often found in philosophy came to seem profoundly sensible to me. In the eighties and early nineties it was an almost exclusively feminist concern to argue that emotion and reason
should not always be opposed, and that emotions might at least sometimes have some cognitive content. These days such an idea is practically
the orthodoxy. Finally, and concerning now the professional practice of
philosophy, the most basic driving intuition among feminist women in
philosophy of that time was, I think, the idea that it can make a difference who is doing the philosophy. Here again, I think that's true. I mean,
the sense in which it's true is completely obvious. Our discipline has a
history, therefore it could have taken a different course. If it had been
as female-dominated as it has de facto been male-dominated, it would
very likely have been different. At least this is a perfectly coherent possibility. Yet even this much acknowledgement of contingency in intellectual activity is suppressed in so many philosophical conversations
of the recognised kind, perhaps because the very thought threatens to
undermine Anglo-American philosophy's self-conception as a universalistic discipline.

Of course our aim is and should be universalistic, if what that amounts
to is a commitment to arguing for things on grounds that anyone could
accept. That is a sound and supremely valuable Enlightenment ideal,
and moreover a semi-realistic aim for those areas where it is sufficiently determinate what anyone should accept. But philosophy as I en-

countered it in those days too often seemed to conflate this aspirational possibility with actuality, transmuting the laudable ideal into an unsaid affirmation of extant philosophy's universalistic achievement. This narcissistic fantasy resulted in the silencing of a most important species of dissent: claims that some philosophical lines of thought reflected a particular point of view or background experience of the world just sounded like gibberish in the face of philosophy's self-image as a definitively universalistic enterprise. This fantasised self-image deep in the philosophical psyche made it seem heretical (no, worse! it made it seem like one was 'missing the point') to protest as a student, If philosophy's so neutral, how come you're still all men?[1]

People talk about loving their subject. I love doing philosophy; though it's more a matter of not being able to help it. In particular, what I can't help is my fascination with philosophy's power of self-deception. (It must be hard being the discipline that remains after all the others have left home to become, variously, physics, biology, chemistry, history, literature, poetry... No wonder it has a continuing identity crisis, a manifest need to explain itself to itself, to affirm just what it is and what it can do—witness recent outpourings of metaphilosophy.) Perhaps that's good. Perhaps it shows that despite being so incredibly old, it is actually still in its adolescence, with plenty of future in which to blossom and own itself. (Maybe, like Orlando, it will turn out less gendered than expected too. Time will tell.) But I realise the onus is on me to explain this therapeutic diagnosis that philosophy has a tendency to self-deception. In truth I think the tendency runs deep in the character of our discipline: philosophy as we know it is intrinsically given to self-deception—something which, incidentally, makes me like it much more than I do when it appears untroubled, unassailably confident in its universalistic achievement. For it is given to self-deception because of its laudable and essential Enlightenment aspiration, combined with the manifest fact of its historical situatedness. Here's another way of putting it. I did Philosophy and French as an undergraduate, and the contrast with literature allowed me to see, as I believed I did, that the philosophy I was being educated in has somehow repressed the knowledge that it's a text. Why? Perhaps the knowledge would threaten to reveal that, like all texts, philosophy has an implied reader. This risky truth threatens to reveal an implied reader who is not the boasted universal 'anyone' after all. Philosophy's concerns might be revealed as universal merely in form, concealing a shamefully parochial content.

---

[1] Not all, but still today a great majority. For recent figures in the UK, see Women in Philosophy in the UK: A report by the British Philosophical Association and the Society for Women in Philosophy UK, authored by Helen Beebee and Jenny Saul (Sept 2011).

There should be no shame in being parochial in that sense; but still, my impression then was that this was a manifest truth that philosophy found threatening. Texts occur in history, and there's something deep in the psyche of Anglo-American philosophy that is still in denial about having a history. One way of talking about what the advent of feminist philosophy meant is to say that feminists asked philosophy to confront the fact that it is a text, so that the uninvited figures of author, narrator, implied reader and real reader all crowd into the space in which we are trained to pretend need make room only for a rational being or two.

Insofar as philosophy generates or aims at knowledge, then all of the above not only tells a story that happens to explain why I was personally drawn to social epistemology. More importantly the story points to a pair of questions that constitute a central project in social epistemology: How is philosophical knowledge generated, and how far are the current practices good ones? I don't know the answer to these questions, but I look at the figures and I worry that things aren't as different from when I started out as I can be tempted to imagine them to be. In this I catch myself in the grip of the very fantasy I have attributed to our discipline. No surprise there. It is the nature of the beast. That's something for which I now have my part in a collective professional responsibility, and while there are no quick fixes, there are things we can do. Some of them concern the content of the philosophy we write: Doing social epistemology in a way that draws attention to the contingencies and possible injustices in what is recognised as knowledge, or as rational, or as interesting, represents a tiny but real impetus in a progressive direction. Or so I would like to believe.

2. What are your main contributions to the field of social epistemology?

I hope to have said something useful about the significant overlap between epistemology and ethics. This overlap was the subject matter of my work on epistemic injustice. It concerns possibilities for people to wrong each other specifically as epistemic subjects: a hearer may wrong a speaker, for instance, by allowing prejudice to depress the level of credibility given (testimonial injustice); or people may be epistemically wronged in a structural way by being situated in a way that is structurally unfair in respect of their participation as epistemic subjects (hermeneutical marginalisation) and consequent ability to make sense of their social experiences (hermeneutical injustice). I suppose my hope is that in opening up the theoretical space of epistemic injustice I might have made certain philosophical thoughts more articulable for those who want to pursue further possibilities.

In effect I hope to have integrated certain feminist insights into epistemology in a way that implicitly makes plain that they belong there. In particular I hope to have shown that it can pay philosophical dividends to look at our epistemic practices from the point of view of those on the losing end. More generally, I hope to have convinced at least some people of the view that one useful sense of 'social' in social epistemology is a lot more than just doing epistemology in a way that has more than one individual in its purview. Rather the 'social' in social epistemology can usefully be a fully socialised conception of the epistemic subject: someone necessarily placed in, and operating under the constraints of, social relations of power and identity; and necessarily placed in time too, so that diachronic aspects of epistemic practices may come to light. In eschewing individualism, social epistemology expands the philosophical point of view so that it can take in collective strategies for achieving knowledge and sharing ideas, and collective strategies are not only socially but also temporarily extended.

3. What is the proper role of social epistemology in relation to other disciplines?

I simply believe that different kinds of social epistemology can help forge links—common questions, common methods, an expansion of the critical repertoire—with neighbouring disciplines. Just as formal social epistemology, or more empirical social epistemology helps cultivate positive intellectual relations with psychology and the social sciences, my hope would be that the kind of social epistemology I do might help forge links with neighbouring humanities such as history, literature, and also law.

One of the ways that social epistemology can do this—though I would emphasize this is not the only way—is to adopt an aim that is normally the province of literature: that of being well observed. The writer who is a great observer of human life produces works that are psychologically insightful, perceptive, and truthful in the imaginative sense of being true to life. Might this not be a proper aim of at least some kinds of philosophy?

One way of doing this depends on adopting different philosophical methods. Our default method is conceptual analysis. But it should not be a default that's adopted thoughtlessly, for it is far more limiting to the philosophical enterprise than we normally allow. First there is the relatively obvious thought that if the concept or practice that we want to explain philosophically is a family concept in the Wittgensteinian sense, then manifestly any attempt at analysis is doomed to failure (though we may learn plenty along the way). But what is far less obvious is that there might be cases—perhaps many cases—of concepts or practices that do permit of analysis, but whose most characteristic and explanatorily fundamental features are not quite necessary conditions. So these all-important features cannot earn a place in our definition. Where this is so, the strict definition of the concept or practice will not describe the basic or paradigm case. And so when we do, finally, end the trial by counter-example, at last to stand back and view the residue of our clever inquisition, what we find is something very small, composed of fewer elements than a paradigm case would be. An essence of sorts, but an essence composed of elements jointly sufficient only for some highly atypical cases of the phenomenon we actually want to understand.

If, on the other hand, we reflect more explicitly than we normally do upon what sort of philosophical understanding we actually want to achieve, then we may be able to develop alternatives to conceptual analysis that may serve us better on some occasions. One kind of possibility here is State of Nature explanations, a sub-class of genealogical explanations (the sub-class that does posit an original position whose features are thereby argued to be in some way necessary for the concept or practice whose origins we are aiming to display). This method seems to me a very natural one to use in social epistemology, in the rather minimal sense that a characteristic feature of the State of Nature is that it contains more than one person.

But this is not the only method. A related, and perhaps less cumbersome one is simply to let the social imagination go to work a little more than usual, and hazard a guess at what elements of a given concept or practice strike one as basic in the here and now. (This is actually what most State of Nature stories do too, only their narrative form creates endless possibilities for confusion about whether or how far one is making an as-if historical claim, a real historical claim, or a daring synchronic claim about the present content of the concept or the function of the practice. This muddies the waters in a way that is often unhelpful.) Once one has hazarded the guess or (as some will prefer) posited the hypothesis, one that is informed by a humanistic sense of the point and purpose of the concept or practice in question, one can go on to test out how far that basic practice is explanatorily prior to other, less basic versions of the practice. Such a method is at least partially on display in P. F. Strawson's approach to explaining the stability of moral responsibility in relation to the apparent threat of determinism. What is most basic, he asserts, in our practices of holding each other responsible (and so presuming each other free in the requisite sense) is the operation of the human 'reactive attitudes'. They are fundamental to a recognisably human mode of interaction, and are in that sense necessary (one might say, original).[2]

---

[2] P. F. Strawson, 'Freedom and Resentment', in Freedom and Resentment and Other

The focus on what is human, and a certain faith in our powers of observation and judgements about what is basic would help make philosophy more of the humanistic discipline it deserves to be.[3] This would re-connect it with its humanistic neighbours who must, at present, stand by wistfully as they observe philosophy play out its enduring crush on the sciences.

4. What have been the most significant advances in social epistemology?

To show that epistemology is not exhausted by attention to individuals, or even relations between individuals as such. More generally, and in relation to my personal intellectual priorities, what I find most significant is the breadth of reference that social epistemology has effectively achieved, spanning formal epistemology, some of feminist epistemology, and as I will suggest below, collective epistemology. I think that the category 'social epistemology' is incredibly progressive in this way, and it has allowed more different voices to become intelligible to one another.

5. What are the most important open problems in social epistemology and what are the prospects for progress?

Let me point not to individual open problems (of which there are surely many—in fact, aren't they all open? Even the original social epistemological questions such as the epistemology of testimony remain stubbornly open.). Let me point instead to a new and burgeoning area: the epistemology of collectives. The reason why I feel this is such a promising and open field is chiefly its promise of making connections with political philosophy.

This is because political philosophy is interested in the proper institutionalisation of power, and institutional bodies are vitally important collective epistemic subjects—juries, industrial tribunals, governments—so that the propriety or impropriety, functionality or dysfunctionality of real epistemic processes in institutions need to be attended to and understood. But that is not just a question of theorising ideal epistemic practices. The power relations and vested interests at work in the economy of credibility also mean that we need to understand not only what ideal collective epistemic practices are like, but (perhaps first) what the salient risks of dysfunctionality are. How are our epistemic practices

---

Essays (London: Methuen, 1974).

[3] In this connection, see Bernard Williams 'Philosophy As A Humanistic Discipline', in his posthumous collection of the same name, ed. A. W. Moore (New Jersey: Princeton University Press, 2006).

most likely to go wrong in the real world of institutional interactions with other institutional bodies and with individual citizens? We need some social epistemology that is informed by the realpolitik of collective epistemic practices in a way that connects with political philosophy. One sort of connection might be this: if, for instance, citizens suffer epistemic injustices at the hands of a complaints panel, a police force, or an employer, this undermines their power to contest, and on some views thereby compromises their political freedom.[4]

In political philosophy there is a useful distinction between ideal theory and non-ideal theory. I think that in social epistemology what we need is a healthy dose of non-ideal theory. We need more often to inflect our theories with a realistic sense of how things tend to go, how they go wrong, and in particular how they create unfair advantage and disadvantage. And once that picture of things is achieved—perhaps with some interdisciplinary help—it might become clearer what ameliorative measures are required to stabilise our practices for the better. Modelling good institutional epistemic practices (such as sharing information, preserving accurate information, seeking advice, dealing with disagreement, making recommendations, coming to verdicts, and so forth) is something social epistemology should have a hand in, but it should do so, I believe, by paying special attention to risks of dysfunctionality first, remedy second. Philosophy has a tendency to characterise the ideal; I think it is useful, by contrast, to focus on likely failure, most especially on the kind of failure that creates disadvantage.

---

[4] I develop this idea in 'Epistemic Justice as a Condition of Political Freedom', Synthese (March 2013).

7

Steve Fuller

Auguste Comte Chair in Social Epistemology

University of Warwick, UK

---

1. Why were you initially drawn to social epistemology?

As the person who started the first journal and wrote the first book with the title 'social epistemology' (Fuller 1988), there was not much to draw me to the field initially! I had run across the phrase 'social epistemology' in passing while reading Marc De Mey's *The Cognitive Paradigm* in the early 1980s (By the end of the decade, De Mey became the first person that I interviewed for the journal *Social Epistemology*.) However, the proximate cause was Fred Schmitt's call for papers on something specifically called 'social epistemology' in the journal *Synthese*, which I had seen as a Ph.D. student in history and philosophy of science at the University of Pittsburgh in the early 1980s. My Ph.D., completed in 1985 (two years before the special issue of *Synthese* actually appeared), was entitled 'Bounded Rationality in Law and Science'. It dealt with the issues that arise from having to take decisions in the present, the justification of which must be drawn from past cases while at the same time setting precedent for future judgements. My basic strategy, which I still uphold, is to try to understand ordinary scientists as if they were judges making decisions in some jurisdiction. In other words, a scientist should be deciding on the general theory to which she would bind her colleagues – which in turn would mark her judgement as 'scientific' rather than simply personal. That the actual history of science fails to live up to such Kant-inspired standards should come as no surprise, given the local character of normative enforcement. In fact, although I wrote my Ph.D. in a period when consensus theories of truth were quite popular, as a C.S. Peirce revival was afoot (partly from the pragmatic turn in German philosophy *à la* Habermas and Apel, and partly through the efforts of Putnam and Mary Hesse), I always believed that the appearance of consensus in science was an artefact of scientists using much the same (especially mathematical) language but meaning quite different things that only come to the fore during a Kuhn-style 'crisis' in the scientists' paradigm. The interesting question is how science's epistemic reputation for unity is maintained amidst all this *de facto* semantic diversity. (In fact, the only part of my dissertation that I have published – as a chapter of the book *Social Epistemology* – refers to the 'elusiveness' of consensus in science.)

The main answer pursued in my Ph.D. is related to a central theme in my work, namely, the ongoing historical reconstruction of one's self-understanding – what, in the case of science, Kuhn called the 'Orwellian' relationship that scientists have to their past. In other words, the past is adapted to fit the current paradigm, which involves *inter alia* distinguishing central from peripheral research concerns, demarcating proper scientists from non-scientists, etc. — even if the lines are drawn in ways that would not have been recognized by those identified as the precursors of today's scientists. As a graduate student I joined the Society for Social Studies of Science (4S), subscribing to the rather counter-Kuhnian view that the new sociology of scientific knowledge (or 'Edinburgh School') could be seen as re-introducing science's repressed history to challenge the epistemic monopoly of the dominant paradigm. Within a decade that stance would result in the public crisis in scientific authority dubbed the 'Science Wars'. (During my M.Phil. and Ph.D. studies in history and philosophy of science at Cambridge and Pittsburgh the new sociology of science was not well known but my supervisors in each programme – Mary Hesse and J.E. McGuire – included it in their courses.)

It is worth mentioning here that much of the ongoing epistemological discussion about whether science 'aims for the truth' has been misdirected because the interesting disagreements arise less over that question than which truths are worth pursuing and the means by which they are pursued and the resulting claims are to be adjudicated. The rhetoric surrounding science 'aiming for the truth' is an atavism of a collective teleological (e.g. positivist, idealist) approach to knowledge, which while true to James Ferrier's original 19th century coinage of 'epistemology', applies much less today — at least as an *assumption* about the pursuit of knowledge. In its original 19th century context, 'aiming for the truth' meant the ultimate systematic representation of reality, which largely only physicists now continue in their quest for a 'Grand Unified Theory of Everything'. Nevertheless, it does not at all follow that I reject this macro-epistemic project (Fuller 2015). On the contrary, I believe that what had been assumed by Ferrier as a general aim of epistemology now needs to be actively constructed as a project in today's diversified yet globally undirected epistemic world, which incidentally is how I understand the spirit in which logical positivism positioned itself in the normative disarray of Weimar culture (Fuller 2007: chap. 2).

My own social epistemology stands very much in this lineage – one that sees Comte, Hegel and Whewell as early 19th century fellow travelers who contributed to Ferrier's 'epistemology'. (This point helps to explain the naming of my chair – the world's first in 'social epistemology' — after Comte.) If Alvin Goldman understood this point – and perhaps more of the overall drift of the history of thought – he would not so violently mislabel my position as 'veriphobic'. In this respect, I find the recent dispute that has erupted between Goldman (2010) and William Alston (2005) over whether social epistemology is 'real epistemology' to be historically myopic – as if 'epistemology' had not existed prior to, say, Bertrand Russell's *The Problems of Philosophy,* which reduced the general problem of knowledge to the defeat of skepticism. And even in that context Russell granted that we could at least proceed to a scientific understanding of the world by removing the intellectual default positions – dogmas, biases, blind spots — on which skepticism feeds.

2. What are your main contributions to the field of social epistemology?

Generally speaking, my main contributions have been concerned with the overall conceptualization of social epistemology as a field of inquiry and especially the reflexive implications of social epistemology for the ends of knowledge and the normative standing (or 'social role') of the knowledge producer.

The concern with the field's overall conceptualization drove me early in my career to identify the normative orientation of epistemology as such with long-term research and education policy, since only these contexts provide systematic opportunities to re-structure knowledge production as whole. I have seen only a difference of degree (not of kind) between the task of arriving at abstract definitions and criteria for knowledge and that of arriving at legislation to promote research innovation and curricular reform. In this context, I have stood out from others who claim to be 'social epistemologists' in that I have specifically defended the university in the classical Humboldtian sense of an institution that systematically 'creatively destroys' the elite nature of innovative research by making it generally available through public education – that is, the 'unity of research and teaching'. Whether this institution needs to be in one concrete site – i.e. campus-based – or can be 'virtual' in any of a number of different respects, I take to be simply a licence for the Humboldtian imperative to be realized in multiple concrete forms.

While I think there are certain personal advantages in receiving my own sort of 'liberal arts' education, I would not fetishise it. Rather, I would stress the underlying epistemic principle informing the Hum-

boldtian model of the university, namely, that one should seek to eliminate, whenever possible, any form of knowledge that allows one to systematically disadvantage another. The relevant sense of 'elimination'
occurs by developing more efficient means of reaching the same epistemic ends – at least through pedagogy but increasingly automated technology. In this respect, the democratization of knowledge is expanded
by the sort of 'product substitutions' that are characteristic of neo-clas-
sical economics, where 'products' initially realized in abstruse journal
articles are later instantiated in clever teaching techniques and perhaps
even mobile phone applications. Indeed, my own social epistemology
abides by George Bernard Shaw's maxim that expert professions are
by nature a conspiracy against the public interest, and so the easier it
is to break their monopolies and rent-seeking practices, the better. (My
Knowledge Management Foundations has developed this point about
the economics of knowledge production most fully.) The university is
the most hallowed institution explicitly dedicated to that end, which as
a regulative ideal amounts to make all things knowable to everyone.

The last point bears on social epistemology's promotion of an image
of the knowledge producer. In my popular book *The Intellectual*, I
defended a person who is more concerned with *the whole truth* than
only the truth. The intellectual would prefer to utter falsehoods that are
subsequently eliminated, attenuated or mitigated than utter truths that
turn out to prevent the pursuit of further truths, either by declaring an
end to a line of inquiry or threatening that a heterodox line of inquiry
would render the inquirer pathological. In short, overstatement invites
participation from others – however negative the consequences for the
utterer herself – whereas understatement carries what Paul Grice used
to call the 'implicature' that individuals should worry most of all about
their own personal epistemic status. The groundwork for my thinking
along these lines was a training and interest in psychology and rhetoric. Psychology was my minor subject as a Columbia undergraduate,
which had I not won the university's Kellett Fellowship to Cambridge
would have led me to MIT to work with Jerry Fodor in psycholingui-
stics, which was all the rage in the late 70s. (As it turns out, my time at
Cambridge left a permanent impression about the metaphysical depth
of antirealism, especially when understood in broadly social terms, as
in the case of the love-to-hate philosopher *du jour*, Michael Dummett.)
In any case, my early psychology training enabled me as a student at the
University of Pittsburgh to teach the required course in the history and
systems of psychology to undergraduates majoring in the field. I carried
over this interest to early formulations of social epistemology, especially in *Philosophy of Science and Its Discontents*, which led me to

become associated with the effort to establish 'psychology of science' as a distinct field in the science studies disciplines. My interest in this field has always been, I believe, similar to that of Karl Popper (whose Ph.D. was in educational psychology), namely, to arrive at an account of knowledge that acknowledges at once the depth of our natural liabilities and our aspirations to transcend them artificially (aka the scientific method). Also as a graduate student I took courses in rhetoric, which on balance provides a more profound and usable understanding of the 'context' of knowledge production than anything offered by sociology or social studies of science. To this day the full intellectual resources of rhetoric have yet to be exploited, which I can only attribute to the dark shadow that Plato continues to cast over the field. My most extensive exploitation strategy to date is *Philosophy, Rhetoric and the End of Knowledge*, whose most recent edition benefits from the editorial insight and pedagogical suggestions of the current editor of the journal *Social Epistemology*, Jim Collier (Fuller & Collier 2004).

As should be clear from the above, my version of social epistemology has been unique from its inception in conceiving of the field as inherently interdisciplinary, with the specific aim of transforming epistemology. This intent was already present in the subtitle of the journal *Social Epistemology* — 'knowledge, culture and policy' — which I proposed to Taylor & Francis while waiting for my Ph.D. viva in 1985. In my original formulation, SE is what epistemology looks like once it takes the history and social studies of science 'seriously', in the sense of having them provide empirical constraints within which epistemic norms can be constructed. However, while associating this project with the 'naturalistic' turn in the philosophy of science, I have always believed (and articulated most explicitly in *Philosophy of Science and Its Discontents*) that naturalism needs to be understood 'reflexively', by which I mean that one consequence of understanding science as a natural outgrowth of the human condition is that we may conclude that naturalism cannot explain the actual motivation and/or the success of science. About ten years ago I learned that this point is not original to me but had been made in T.H. Huxley's 1893 Romanes Lecture, 'Evolution and Ethics'. In a nutshell, Huxley argued that had Darwin preceded Newton, Newton would never have happened because Darwin's desacralized and epistemically diminished conception of the human condition would have rendered preposterous the Newtonian aspiration to understand the entire universe from the standpoint of some divine creator. Indeed, Huxley wondered how the pursuit of science would be motivated in the 20th century, once Darwinism becomes part of both popular and scientific self-understanding.

Whereas Huxley ended on a concerned, if not pessimistic, note about the fate of large scale, long term human enterprises that are dedicated in defiance of natural selection, not least science, I conclude on the basis of much the same analysis that it is a serious mark against Darwinism that all it can say about the most distinctive features of the human condition is that they are temporary by-products of evolutionary processes fundamentally indifferent to our fate. In other words, Darwinism fails to take sufficiently seriously that a trained-up version of *Homo sapiens* may be sufficiently different from our animal antecedents to overcome or at least master the forces of nature by coming to understand how they work. At first glance, this conclusion looks like the epistemic state that compelled Kant to postulate God, as well as unity and purpose in nature, as a regulative condition of inquiry. And perhaps this was my starting intuition, but I have moved away from Kant's original metaphysically minimalist ('as if') spirit. I now believe that the progress of science (most of which has happened since Kant's time) has converted these regulative conditions into achievable goals, such that by the very activity of science we realize them. You might say that while I am reasonably considered a 'constructivist' (rather than, say, a 'realist'), it would be more accurate to describe my position as 'realizationist' (rather than, say, 'relativist'). In other words, I believe that we increasingly come to turn into reality whatever we conceive, which I am also inclined to interpret as a sign of our self-deification – as in a rather literal sense of the Biblical idea that we are created *imago dei*. The very important open question for social epistemology is the set of beings to which 'we' and 'our' applies (Fuller & Lipinska 2014).

3. What is the proper role of social epistemology in relation to other disciplines?

The arch Popperian Joseph Agassi once described the philosopher as the scientist's backseat driver. While he meant this in his characteristically ironic way (i.e. the recipient of one's advice might be less than appreciative, even if turned out to be have well taken), I fear that analytic social epistemologists take the self-description in a rather more po-faced way, supposing that it is simply enough to say that some knowledge-relevant procedure, situation or practice would be better were it to go (or have gone) this or that way, regardless of how the advice is likely to be received. It is as if the analytic social epistemologist were primarily concerned with assuaging her own conscience (i.e. 'I said the right thing') rather than with making a positive material difference to the practices of those whom she would instruct. My interest in the latter has led me to study and promote the psychology and rhetoric of science as integral to any practically credible social epistemology, which I believe should recognise the 'conventionality' of disciplinary boundaries in two senses of the term – not only that they are there to be transcended but also that they are often treated as irreversible foundations.

I believe that philosophy may relate to interdisciplinarity in two distinct ways: On the one hand, it may play an auxiliary role in the process of intedisciplinarity, typically through conceptual analysis, in the understanding that the disciplines themselves are the main epistemic players. This version of the relationship I characterise as 'normal' because it captures the more common pattern of the relationship, reflecting an acceptance of the division of organized inquiry into disciplines. On the other hand, philosophy may be itself the site for the production of interdisciplinary knowledge, understood as a kind of second-order understanding of reality that transcends the sort of knowledge that the disciplines provide, left to their own devices. This is my own position, which I dub 'deviant' (Fuller 2013). Underlying the two types are contrasting notions of what constitutes the 'efficient' pursuit of knowledge. Normal interdisciplinarity interprets the relevant sense of 'efficiency' in terms of following the path of least resistance, which in this context means making the most use of the knowledge resources already available, as, say, dictated by the logic of puzzle-solving in Kuhnian normal science. In contrast, deviant interdisciplinarity is more concerned with finding more efficient means of reaching comparable or superior epistemic ends, which at the limit would allow anyone to know everything. The foundational character of philosophy in the modern ('Humboldtian') university derives from this latter image, which was most imaginatively developed by the German idealists following Kant. To be sure, the normal/deviant distinction was already marked in the institution's medieval origins in terms of the difference between Doctors and Masters, respectively, an artefact of which remains in the postgraduate/undergraduate degree distinction, especially if we associate the former with 'expertise' or 'profession' and the latter 'liberal arts'.

4. What have been the most significant advances in social epistemology?

It is difficult to say whether social epistemology has made major advances in terms of substantially altering knowledge practices for the better. (Yes, a lot of stuff has been published in the past 25 years – but who cares?) The time horizon may be too short for a measured judgement, though I would offer the ideas, arguments and conclusions raised in this interview as candidate for 'advances'.

However, I do not believe that analytic social epistemology has made significant advances, despite the number of articles and books published in the area, mainly because of its 'minimalist' aspirations in the following respects: (1) a tendency to operate with a minimal under-standing of actual knowledge practices, including their histories and aspirations, a strategy that is often defended in the name of maximum abstraction and generality; (2) a tendency to minimize the impact that the philosopher could have on ongoing forms of inquiry, such that the Lockean self-description of having been an 'underlabourer' for Newton is presented as ambitious; (3) a tendency to focus on extant epistemic practices – 'trust', 'testimony', 'expertise' — that appear designed so as to minimally upset the status quo, such that those who would signifi-cantly alter our default epistemic behaviours are always put on the back foot in terms of burden of proof.

5. What are the most important open problems in social epistemology and what are the prospects for progress?

Perhaps the most important overarching problem for social epistemo-logy is the relationship between so-called *moral* and *epistemic* values. Although several different characterizations have been given of this re-lationship, generally speaking either (1) epistemic values are cast as a special case of moral values or (2) moral values are portrayed as placing constraints on the realization of epistemic values. In the case of (1), epistemic values are envisaged as a kind of 'ethics of belief', to recall the title of W.K. Clifford's 1877 lecture, which famously defined intel-lectual discipline as 'belief proportional to evidence'. In recent times, a broadened conception of 'epistemic virtue' that harks back to Ari-stotle and Aquinas rather than Bacon and Mach has taken root in social epistemology, which is more focused on character-based values of the epistemic agent, such as honesty, humility, open-mindedness, tolerance, etc. In the case of (2), epistemic values are portrayed as potentially undermining of the human condition if they are not pursued within a certain ethical horizon. This orientation conjures up the spectre of the morally indifferent if not inhuman scientist, who in turn requires the oversight of institutional review boards, if not natural law-based restric-tions on scientific experiments on human and animals.

My own preferred view, introduced in the final chapter of *The So-ciology of Intellectual Life*, involves taking Ockham's Razor to the di-stinction between moral and epistemic value by arguing that their real difference lies in the time horizon within which a more generic sense of 'value' is expected to be fully realized. Specifically, so-called 'epi-stemic value' operates with a much longer time horizon for realizing the same sense of 'value' as that of so-called 'moral value'. Here I am identifying 'epistemic value' with the pursuit of truth as an end in itself, which is to say, regardless of the means pursued to achieve it (which in practice amounts to an ethic of efficiency). And given both my associating social epistemology with the original collective teleological project of 'epistemology' and the more recent development of 'post-' and 'trans-' human normative horizons, whereby the values that humans have traditionally tried to achieve come to be realized in some successor 'species', I have come to believe that we should take seriously the claim of extreme scientists – including Nazi ones – that their research aims to benefit the human condition, despite possibly harming many humans in the short-to-medium term.

Of course, it does not follow that we should automatically let them do what they wish but we should not pre-empt the normative validity of their claims by demonizing them as 'pathological', 'inhumane', etc. After all, precedent for the long-termist, 'end justifies the means' ethic of extreme scientists may be found in utilitarian arguments for the welfare of future generations, which would have people discount or deny the value of their own current pleasures in favour of imagined future ones that may well be experienced by others rather than by oneself. This argument is used to justify the systematic redistribution of various resources away from their default users and uses. The salient difference between this and the epistemic value case is (so I maintain) that the latter is effectively a second-order version of the former. In other words, sacrificing part of the current population to benefit some indefinitely extended future population is like sacrificing a part of one's current self to benefit either a future version of oneself or some future being whose values are sufficiently similar to one's own.

I believe that it is only for historical reasons that the relationship between moral and epistemic value has not been seen in this way. In particular, past cases of the dominance of 'epistemic value' (e.g. eugenics) have been coerced rather than freely chosen by those who would be most likely to suffer the immediate consequences. In the emerging world of what I have called 'Humanity 2.0' political ideologies, I have characterized the second-order, epistemic value-led option as *proactionary* (suggesting a risk-seeking mentality) and the first-order, moral value-led option as *precautionary* (suggesting a risk-averse mentality). However, both presuppose a substantial demand to redistribute personal sentiment and material resources. However, the social-epistemic standpoint of the precautionary ideology is that of those living now who then imagine others who would wish to live like them in the future, as opposed to the proactionary ideology, which envisages future life as involving roughly the same degree of dismissal, incorporation and extension of the past as previous generations have done to their predecessors.

In addition to this overarching question, I would propose four more specific questions for social epistemologists:

- **The Social Epistemology of Philosophy as an Academic Discipline.** Although some important work in this vein has been done on the sociological side by Randall Collins, with contributions by Martin Kusch on the philosophical side, it has been typically undertaken in a purely historical spirit without reflexively applying the insights learned about past episodes to today's organization of philosophical knowledge. (I like to think that my own *Sociology of Intellectual Life* is an exception.) This is a somewhat peculiar state-of-affairs considering that a quarter-century ago, the topic was arguably much hotter, often as critical responses to Richard Rorty's call for philosophy to merge into a more general humanistic discipline equally concerned with history and literature as with logic and science. I suppose the prominence of Brian Leiter – first with his 'Philosophical Gourmet' ranking of philosophy programmes and then with his 'Leiter Reports' blog (the discipline's answer to Fox News) – has provided one sort of closure to this line of inquiry, which perhaps discourages more nuanced approaches. Leiter denies the presence of deep differences in philosophical schools, the recognition of which however would immediately turn the social epistemology of philosophical knowledge into a matter for professional concern: i.e. given that 'analytic' and 'continental' schools have such different *modus operandi*, in what sense can they be considered alternative schools of 'philosophy'? (For his part, Leiter believes that there is only 'good' and 'bad' philosophy, the difference between which emerges from the peer judgements collected together by the likes of his own Philosophical Gourmet.)

  Of course, the very idea that philosophy is *primarily* an academic discipline – especially in the exact same sense as the other academic disciplines (i.e. *not* a second-order discipline or simply a general attitude toward living) – is largely an early 20th century invention. It is customary to declare Kant the first philosopher to earn a living by being a professor, yet his conception of philosophy – as that of his idealist followers and, indeed, most philosophers until after the First World War – was that of a second-order discipline that one studied before entering into first-order, typically empirical disciplines. (This mentality persisted in movements as recent as pragmatism and even logical positivism, both of which had rather polemical relations with theology, the previous pretender to second-order disciplinary status.) In contrast, we can point to (in the Anglophone world) G.E. Moore and (in the Germanophone world) Karl Jaspers as having provided accounts of philosophy as a discipline with its own proper subject matter – the former, 'pre-analytic intuitions'; the latter the history of philosophy itself – that can be studied without reference to anything else. Here we see the germs of the institutional distinction between so-called analytic and continental philosophy that came to be magnified over the 20th century through the alternative pedagogies implied in Moore's and Jaspers' accounts. My own interest in the social epistemology of philosophical knowledge stems from my belief that philosophy lost its way when it became a first-order discipline and that post-positivist analytic-philosophical attempts to recover the discipline's second-order status as 'conceptual underlabourer' to the first-order disciplines is a deformation of the original Kantian impulse, which was to have philosophy provide a sense of unity and purpose to what even in Kant's day (see his *Contest of Faculties*) was academia's increasingly fractious and fractionating disciplinary structure.

- **The Social Epistemology of Default Positions**: A striking feature of much of the work in analytic social epistemology is a tendency to see problems of knowledge as arising from given properties of agents in given situations, without asking how the agents came to be as they are, facing the problems that they do, which in turn calls forth some sort of explicit epistemic activity. At first glance, this assumption, which unites philosophical interests as disparate as Alvin Goldman's and Lorraine Code's, seems harmless and perhaps even necessary, if any systematic social epistemology is to be had. However, such a starting point obscures the fact that an agent's self-understanding is always being influenced, even when she is not aroused to solve a problem that entails asking 'Who should I believe?' In this respect, whatever their conceptual shortcomings, propagandistic and epidemiological models of idea transmission (popularised nowadays by Richard Dawkins as 'meme theory') are to be recommended for drawing attention to the extent to which we are regularly being shaped as epistemic agents, even when we do not choose to be. At one level the point is obvious, but at another level much less so. Throughout the history of philosophy, the epistemic status of, broadly speaking, 'metaphysical' notions has been routinely held under suspicion for promising much but delivering little from an empirical standpoint. However, the persuasiveness of this charge relies on our ignoring whatever influence those notions might have already had in making the epistemic agent who she normally is. In that case, it should not be so surprising that there is little 'value added' epistemically by explicitly believing in such notions. For example, I would submit that this is the sense in which Ockham used his famous razor to underwrite an argument for – rather than against – the existence of God: It provides the simplest explanation for our being the sort of creature we are, one who sees the world in a certain unified, meaningful manner, etc. We nowadays associate this line of reasoning with 'transcendental arguments', but my point here is that there is a social epistemology to be had of how certain beliefs come to provide the default settings (or 'presumptions') in terms of which other beliefs – the typically empirically ones — need to be acquired and are then evaluated. (I first raised this in chap. 4 of *Social Epistemology*.) At the moment the closest that analytic social epistemology comes to taking this proposal seriously is when, say, Alvin Goldman questions the epistemic value of democracy by noting how often its decision-making procedures end up reaching the wrong conclusions, and then wondering whether people might not be trained properly to decide about, say, whether creationism deserves space alongside evolution in science courses. An easier way to make the same point: We instinctively recoil against proposals such as Goldman's – and the still more explicit evolution indoctrination campaigns of Dawkins – because they deploy epistemic means to achieve ontological ends, that is, to render people radically other than they normally are.

- **The Social Epistemology of Cognitive Economy – the Use of Resources to Produce Knowledge:** ASE has had an unfortunate tendency to gravitate to aspects of social science that play to its default intellectual biases. No surprise, then, given its natural tilt towards methodological individualism (i.e. knowledge is sought/had in the first instance by individuals and then aggregated somehow into 'social knowledge'), that ASE has fancied microeconomic models that propose to capture the optimal flow of information, division of cognitive labour, etc. But there is of course the *macro*-economics of knowledge, which is concerned with the overall efficiency of the epistemic enterprise, what Nicholas Rescher (1978) called, with a nod to Charles Sanders Peirce, 'cognitive economy'.

The idea worth developing here is an application of what had been a conceptual innovation in Peirce's day, namely, the principle of diminishing marginal utility. Applied to knowledge production, it suggests that the indefinite pursuit of knowledge – especially under current arrangements – is not an end in itself but only good on a benefit-to-cost basis. In other words, our best epistemic enterprises provide the most cognitive benefit at the lowest cost. This principle was explicitly proposed for science policy by the 'finalization' movement associated Habermas when he ran one of the

Max Planck Institutes over thirty years ago. Their idea was that puzzle solving in Kuhnian normal science eventually suffers from diminishing marginal returns on further investment, and so beyond a certain point, resources should be shifted to fields with better epistemic yields. However, ideas surrounding cognitive economy may be deployed in other ways, e.g. as a principle for the critical evaluation of existing knowledge systems: across the range of national and corporate research systems, the rate of return on investment varies significantly. The US may by far produce the most science but the UK is much more productive relative to resource allocation. A comparable point may be made about educational systems. Harvard and Oxford may produce the most impressive roster of graduates but then they also have the most impressive intake of students. The added value, cognitively speaking, of attending these institutions is probably much less than universities operating with fewer resources that nevertheless produce distinguished graduates out of students of humbler origins. It is worth stressing that the main value associated with cognitive economy is best measured in terms of the opportunity costs that can be minimised or avoided, as efficiency savings make more resources available for other projects. The underlying intuition is that one acts now so as to maximise the degree of freedom that is later at one's disposal. In *The Governance of Science*, I spoke of this as 'epistemic fungibility'.

- **The Social Epistemology of Cognitive Economy – the Use of Knowledge Already Produced:** Not only is there a question of whether resources are used efficiently in the production of knowledge but also whether the knowledge so produced is used efficiently. About 25 years ago, the library and information scientist Don Swanson (1986) managed to understand the aetiology of a disease simply by reading across literatures in various fields (which the specialists themselves had not done) and piecing together a hypothesis that was then empirically vindicated by a targeted experiment. Swanson had been motivated by various bibliometric facts of the sort originally highlighted by the science historian Derek de Solla Price in the 1960s, namely, that an exaggerated version of the so-called Pareto 80/20 principle operates in science such that 90% of the citations accrue to 10% of the authors. Sociologists have tended to follow Robert Merton in concluding that the uncited articles are either truly worthless or eventually incorporated into the cited articles, which in turn has led to institutional incentives for scientists to publish in 'high impact' journals or team up with people whose work is already well cited. Swanson thought otherwise: given the lack of evidence that the uncited articles were actually read, he concluded that they were simply neglected and may well contain valuable knowledge. But this would require a change in scientific reading habits so that they are not so strongly focussed on the dominant research tendencies in the specific fields where the research was published, in terms of which the uncited pieces no doubt seem irrelevant. Rather, scientists would have to learn to read across fields to make the connections where the uncited pieces appear as relevant to some other set of problems. An ambitious follow-up to the Swanson result would involve re-deploying research agencies so that they allocate funds, in the first instance, to academics who try to solve standing intellectual and social problems by combing and combining the existing literature, followed by the commissioning of targeted first-order research aimed at testing knowledge claims the validity of which cannot be agreed simply from a comprehensive and measured reading of that literature.

References

Alston, W. 2005. Beyond Justification: Epistemic Dimensions of Evaluation. Ithaca NY: Cornell University Press.

Fuller, S. 1988. Social Epistemology. Bloomington IN: Indiana University Press.

Fuller, S. 2007. New Frontiers in Science and Technology Studies. Cambridge UK: Polity.

Fuller, S. 2013. 'Deviant interdisciplinarity as philosophical practice: Prolegomena to deep intellectual history'. Synthese 190: 1899-1916.

Fuller, S. 2015. Knowledge: The Philosophical Quest in History. London: Routledge.

Fuller, S. and Collier, J. 2004. Philosophy, Rhetoric and the End of Knowledge. 2nd edn. (Orig. 1993, by Fuller). Mahwah NJ: Lawrence Erlbaum Associates.

Fuller, S. and Lipinska, V. 2014. The Proactionary Imperative. London: Palgrave Macmillan.

Goldman, A. 2010. 'Why social epistemology is real epistemology'. In Haddock, A.; Millar, A. and Pritchard, D., eds. Social Epistemology. Oxford: Oxford University Press, pp. 1-28.

Rescher, N. 1978. Peirce's Philosophy of Science. South Bend IN: University of Notre Dame Press.

Swanson, D. 1986. 'Undiscovered Public Knowledge'. Library Quarterly 56 (2): 103-18

8

Sandy Goldberg

Professor and Chair, Department of Philosophy
Northwestern University

---

1. Why were you initially drawn to social epistemology?

I was initially drawn to social epistemology from a prior interest in the epistemology of testimony. In thinking about testimony I became curious about the other ways in which we rely epistemically on others, including the systematic (social or institutional) efforts that are made to shape our epistemic environments. And once I was thinking of these things, I was well on the way to seeing the pervasiveness of social factors in the acquisition and spread of knowledge.

2. What are your main contributions to the field of social epistemology?

I am not sure that I can speak authoritatively about this, but I am happy to speculate. I would guess that the contributions of mine that have received the most attention include work on four topics: the epistemology of testimony; "coverage-based" beliefs; the division of epistemic labor; and the ways in which social factors in epistemology require a re-thinking of several individualistic assumptions in traditional epistemology. In many of my discussions of these topics I adopt a process reliabilist framework, according to which the epistemic goodness or badness of a belief is determined by the reliability of the processes through which it was formed and sustained. Part of what I suspect are my main contributions consist in showing how a reliabilist framework can be used to model the social phenomena, and how doing so will have implications for how we ought to develop process reliabilism itself.

I begin with my work on testimony. Perhaps the main issue of debate in this area concerns whether the considerations that render a testimonial belief justified are epistemically distinctive. The traditional answer, attributed to Hume, is negative: he held that the considerations in question boil down (or "reduce") to considerations of perception and induction. Opposed to such a "reductionist" view is a position according to which our reliance on testimony is akin to our reliance on other "epistemically basic" sources such as perception. On this view, in the same way that a subject need not justify her reliance on her own perceptual system in order to arrive at justified perceptual belief – in this sense perception is an "epistemically basic" source – so too a subject need not justify his reliance on another's testimony in order to arrive at justified testimonial belief. Such "anti-reductionist" views are usually formulated as advancing a presumptive but defeasible epistemic right to rely on the source in question (perception; another's testimony).

Most of my contributions to the testimony literature have focused on this debate between the reductionist and the anti-reductionist. First, I have argued (in my book Anti-Individualism) that an anti-reductionist view can be defended within the framework of a reliabilist epistemology, and that the resulting view makes plain why one might think of testimony as an "epistemically basic" source akin to perception. Second, I have argued (in "Monitoring and Anti-Reductionism in the Epistemology of Testimony") that when one motivates anti-reductionism in a reliabilist fashion, one can defend the position against Lizzie Fricker's familiar charge that it sanctions gullibility. Third, I have argued (in "Reductionism and the Distinctiveness of Testimonial Knowledge") that the reductionism/anti-reductionism debate does not bear in the way most people suppose on the question whether testimonial knowledge is epistemically distinctive. Most people have supposed that testimonial knowledge is epistemically distinctive if but only if there are testimony-specific epistemic principles – that is, if but only if there is something like a presumptive but defeasible right to accept another's testimony (as anti-reductionism maintains). However, I argue that testimonial knowledge is distinctive whatever the eventual outcome of the reductionism/anti-reductionism debate; my case for the distinctiveness of testimonial knowledge employs premises that should be endorsed even by those who endorse reductionism. On the view I defend, this distinctness consists in the entitlement to "pass the epistemic buck" to the source speaker: when asked about what renders his belief knowledge, a hearer whose knowledge is testimony-based is entitled to direct this query to the source speaker herself. The phenomenon of epistemic buck-passing reveals to us that that testimonial knowledge is essentially social in at least one way: the epistemic support that renders the hearer knowledgeable is possessed, not by the hearer himself, but by his source.

Not all of my work on testimony focuses on the reductionism/anti-reductionism debate, however. In subsequent work I have been more interested in capturing the social dimensions of testimony. It turns out that these go far beyond questions of epistemic buck-passing.

In my book Relying on Others, I adopted a process reliabilist framework in order to argue that traditional process reliabilism has been
too individualistic in its orientation, and must be modified if it is to be
adequate to the epistemology of testimony. If correct this result would
be surprising for two reasons. First, the father of reliabilist epistemology, Alvin Goldman, is also the person most responsible for the recent emergence of interest in social epistemology, and it is surprising to
learn that the father of social epistemology endorses an epistemological
view that is not sufficiently social in orientation. Second, reliabilism
itself emerged out of a wholesale criticism of traditional "internalist"
epistemology, with its focus on what is accessible to the reflecting subject, and it is surprising that a view which recognized the need to move
past the reflections of the individual subject nevertheless continues to
ignore the social dimensions of knowledge. But surprising or not, this
was my claim: process reliabilism was still wedded to an unfortunate
kind of individualism. Whereas any process reliabilist will have to be
committed to the idea that epistemic goodness is a matter of the reliability of belief-forming and sustaining processes, traditional (orthodox)
reliabilism made a further – and to my mind, unnecessary and unfortunate – assumption, to the effect that all such processes are processes
that take place within the mind/brain of a single individual. As against
this, I developed and defended what I called the "extendedness hypothesis." According to this hypothesis, the process by which one's belief
is formed, when one's belief is formed through acceptance of another's
testimony, should be seen as interpersonally extended: it includes not
only the (comprehension- and credibility-monitoring) processes in the
mind/brain of the hearer, but also the processes through which the source speaker herself came to acquire and transmit the information in her
testimony. Although this hypothesis is put in terms of a reliabilist orientation, the same point might be put in other terms as well: the reasons
or evidence that render a hearer's testimonial belief knowledgeable are
those possessed by the speaker. (A version of the latter sort can be seen
in Fred Schmitt's paper, "Testimonial Justification and Transindividual
Reasons.")

Both my "epistemic buck-passing" model of testimony and my "extendedness hypothesis" highlight one instance of a phenomenon that
we might call the "division of epistemic labor." In particular, if you
know through another's testimony, it is her evidence (her reasons; her
reliability) that renders you knowledgeable. We can put the same point
another way: you depend directly on her evidence (reasons; reliability)
for your knowledge and justified belief, in the sense that if she lacks
adequate evidence (reasons; reliability), you fail to know/your belief

fails to enjoy doxastic justification. This is a way in which testimonial knowledge contrasts with other sorts of knowledge, since in other cases you depend only on your own evidence (or reasons or reliability), not on others' evidence (or reasons or reliability), for justified belief and knowledge.

Nor are these the only ways in which testimony cases can help us think about the division of epistemic labor. In two subsequent papers I explored two additional ways.

In "The Social Diffusion of Epistemic Warrant and Rationality," I argued that, in order to appreciate other ways in which we depend epistemically on others in testimony cases, we need to expand our focus beyond the speaker and the hearer. Some background can bring this out. To begin, consider that if the testimonies one accepts are predominantly false or unreliable, this would seem to tell against the reliability with which one distinguishes good (reliable) from bad (unreliable) testimony. If we call this task (of discerning good from bad testimony) the task of managing the flow of information in one's environment, we can then say that how well-off a hearer's testimonial belief is, epistemically speaking, depends on how well he manages the flow of information in his environment: if he is gullible, and so accepts anything others tell him, he will end up accepting a good deal that is false, and such a subject can hardly be credited with doxastically justified testimonial belief. But now consider that the epistemic task avoiding the acceptance of false or unreliable testimonies is easier or harder to the degree that one's environment is less or more full of false or unreliable testimonies. It is here that we see another social dimension of our epistemic reliance on others in testimony cases: insofar as each of us is doing a good job in managing the flow of information around us, so that we accept a preponderance of true testimonies (and reject a preponderance of the false ones), we do our job to keep the epistemic environment "clean." At the very least we are not spreading false testimony; and if speakers who do spread false testimony are rejected enough, perhaps many of them will become discouraged from testifying to those falsities in the future – whether because they begin to doubt their own testimonies, or because they want to avoid being known as unreliable. If we are effective at weeding out false or unreliable testimonies, each of us is playing the role of a "filter", and so each of us helps to increase the percentage in our community of testimonies that are true – thereby making it easier for each one of us to manage the flow of information oneself. Here, then, is another way we epistemically rely on others in our community: we depend on others (as they depend on us) to "police" the flow of information in our community, and in this way to decrease the burden on each of us as individuals, as we seek to ensure against the acceptance of false or unreliable testimonies. In a follow-up paper entitled "The Division of Epistemic Labor," I contrasted this kind of reliance on others with the sort that emerges from a restricted focus on the hearer and speaker alone; I described the former as a "diffuse" kind of reliance, and the latter as a "direct" kind of reliance.

There is yet another way in which testimony cases highlight a division of epistemic labor. The phenomenon in question is best seen in connection with a problem that arises in the consumption of testimony by cognitively immature children. Empirical research suggests that while cognitively immature children between the ages of 2 and 4 are not entirely credulous, they have neither the cognitive sophistication nor the background information with which to reliably discern the credibility of incoming testimony. But most epistemologists assume that a hearer who is unreliable in discerning when testimony is reliable is not justified in accepting the testimonies she does accept. Putting these two points together, we would reach the conclusion that cognitively immature children are not justified in accepting testimony. Assuming (what is plausible) that testimonial knowledge implies justified acceptance, we would reach the further conclusion that cognitively immature children cannot acquire knowledge through testimony. But this conclusion has struck many as simply false. In "Testimonial Knowledge in Early Childhood, Revisited," I argued that this problem is best addressed, once again, by widening our focus beyond the hearer (the immature child) and the testifier. My claim was that in a great many cases, the child's adult guardians provide the protection (against unreliable testimony) that the child cannot provide for himself. The child's guardians do so, first, by structuring the child's environment so that fewer unreliable testimonies reach his ears; and second, by monitoring those testimonies that do reach the child's ears when they (the guardians) are present. In this manner, the child's consumption of testimony is more reliable – a greater preponderance of the testimonies she accepts are true – than her cognitive immaturity alone would lead us to suppose. In subsequent paper ("Testimonial knowledge from unsafe testimony"), I suggested analogues for the case of adult consumers of testimony. If this is correct, it suggests that our epistemic reliance on others in testimony cases can take yet another form.

My work on testimony lead me to think about yet another form of epistemic reliance which, while not testimonial, is intimately related to our reliance on others as testifiers. In particular, we rely on others to provide "coverage" of important news. If asked whether weapons of mass destruction (WMDs), whose alleged presence in Iraq was the pretext for the US invasion of Iraq under President George W. Bush, were ever discovered, you would probably respond in the negative. If asked for the basis on which you think this, you might well respond that, well, if they had been discovered, you would have heard about it by now. I have argued that this sort of belief – formed on the basis of an inference from a lack of testimony on a topic on which one would have expected relevant information to reach one, had there been any such information – is pervasive. In my book Relying on Others, I explore the epistemology of this sort of belief, and I compare and contrast this sort of epistemic reliance to that found in straight testimony cases.

Reflection of these and other sorts of epistemic reliance on others has convinced me that the traditional, individualistic orientation of epistemology is inappropriate, and cannot do justice to the range of beliefs we form through relying on others. In this way I have been lead to reject various orthodoxies in epistemology in general, but also in reliabilist epistemology in particular.

3. What is the proper role of social epistemology in relation to other disciplines?

Since social epistemology is still in its infancy, it has yet to benefit in a systematic way from the various other (theoretical, experimental, or applied) disciplines that examine the flow of information in group or institutional settings. These include psychology, sociology, economics (signaling theory), biology (animal communication systems), as well as such applied areas as law (legal testimony and legal responsibility), business (information generation and information flow in team settings), and education (best practices). I would hope that as it matures, social epistemology takes the best of what these others disciplines has to offer, and contributes in turn to model-building that might be usefully applied to research results from these disciplines.

4. What have been the most significant advances in social epistemology?

In my experience, the most significant advances in social epistemology would probably have to be in the area of testimony. However, there have been interested advances as well in our understanding of group belief (and judgment aggregation).

5. What are the most important open problems in social epistemology and what are the prospects for progress?

I think one of the most important open questions – or rather, one of the most important collection of questions – in social epistemology concerns our reliance (in belief-formation) on instruments or mechanisms (clocks, thermometers, computers, and so forth). I regard this as an important topic, since it goes to the heart of epistemology (and speaks to our nature as epistemic subjects); and I regard this set of questions as open, since I think it is only recently that we understand our reliance on other epistemic subjects (e.g. in testimony cases) well enough to have a useful comparison with our reliance on instruments.

The questions in this set are many. Perhaps the most central one is this: should our reliance on instruments be conceived on the model of our reliance on other speakers, or should we instead regard instruments as we regard any other element of the physical (nonmental) world? Since we can't pass the epistemic buck to a mere instrument, reliance on them seems to be unlike reliance on another speaker; but since they are typically designed to display information regarding the world, they can be assessed, as we assess speakers, in terms of the reliability of the processes by which they produce their representations. In short, we seem to be pulled in both directions.

Interestingly, I think many of the other questions that arise in connection with the epistemology of instrument-based belief are perhaps only partly epistemological. For example: (1) What relevant differences, if any, exist between people (as epistemic subjects) and instruments? (This question is as much metaphysics as epistemology.) (2) Expanding our focus, what is the nature of the sort of reliance exhibited by the one who uses an instrument on the various people who are responsible for the construction and upkeep of the instrument? (Here I think a comparison to the legal responsibilities of those responsible for the construction and upkeep of instruments would be interesting.) (3) How, if at all, does our reliance on instruments change the nature of our epistemic environments? How do the existing structures and institutions in our epistemic environment shape the nature and extent of our reliance on instruments? And what effect(s), if any, do these interrelations have on the epistemology of the corresponding beliefs? (At least some of these questions have a clear sociological dimension.)

I would be remiss to say that these questions have never been addressed; but I think further study is called for, and I see this as one of the more important and exciting parts of social epistemology. I would surmise that the prospects for progress are good.

9

Alvin I. Goldman

Professor of Philosophy and Cognitive Science
Rutgers, The State University of New Jersey

---

1. Why were you initially drawn to social epistemology?

I was never "drawn" to social epistemology — as a pre-existing subject — because it did not exist when I started thinking about it. Even after I began thinking about it, the thoughts needed time to germinate. In 1967 I published "A Causal Theory of Knowing" (Goldman 1967), and in the early 1970s continued writing about knowledge in a causal-psychological-naturalistic vein. Counterfactual, reliabilist, and anti-luck accounts of knowledge were sprouting in the 1970s, one of which was my paper "Discrimination and Perceptual Knowledge" (Goldman 1976), first presented at the Chapel Hill colloquium in 1972. A bit later, in 1975-76, I spent a year at the Center for Advanced Study in the Behavioral Sciences, hatching a plot for a book that would develop these and related epistemological themes I was ruminating about. Some were directed toward social epistemological issues.

Relativism, post-modernism, and social constructivism were blooming at this time. Kuhn's (1962) work had incited a more social orientation toward science, which was adopted by the "Strong Programme" in the sociology of science. In France Foucault's ideas gained prominence. Rorty published his "Philosophy and the Mirror of Nature" (Rorty 1979), which endorsed a number of these ideas. He pronounced the death of epistemology and urged its replacement by a "conversation of mankind." All putative attempts to obtain "truth" were derided as fruitless or confused. These debunkings of classical epistemology left me — like most working epistemologists — utterly unconvinced. My own epistemological bent, as indicated, was reliabilist or "veritistic." Believing the true as opposed to the false was seen as a pervasive aim, and knowledge and justification were to be analyzed in terms of reliable (i.e., truth-getting) methods of belief formation (Goldman 1979). On the other hand, a turn toward the social also seemed attractive. Transparently, social factors have causal influences on intellectual life and belief. But the relativists, social constructivists, historicists, etc. seemed to think (for one reason or another) that the social character of cognitive activity is inimical either to the existence of truth or its attainability. This, in my judgment, was their fundamental error. I saw no reason why epistemology could not be socialized — to an appropriate degree — without abandoning the integrity of truth or its prospects for attainment (under suitable circumstances). Classical epistemology would be preserved, but it would have two branches: an individual-centered branch and a social branch. Social factors need not militate against the truth; well designed social practices might even enhance a community's truth-getting prospects. Having crystallized in my mind the basic idea of a truth-oriented social epistemology, I briefly mentioned this theme in two publications (Goldman 1978, 1986), but these works were principally devoted to individual epistemology.[1] A full development of the social branch took another decade to develop.

2. What are your main contributions to the field of social epistemology?

After returning from my year at the Center for Advanced Study in 1976, at least one of the epistemology courses I gave at the University of Michigan (my home institution at the time) covered some social epistemological themes. As I recollect it, Fred Schmitt encountered these themes in such a course.[2] Schmitt went on to organize and edit the first journal issue (in Synthese) on "classically" or "analytically" oriented social epistemology (Schmitt 1987). This issue appeared in the same year that Steve Fuller's journal, Social Epistemology, was launched, a journal devoted to what I would call "anti-classical" social episte-

---

[1]   In the 1978 paper, "Epistemics: The Regulative theory of Cognition," I wrote as follows: "Actually my conception of epistemics is broader than these remarks suggest. It would comprehend *social* as well as *individual* dimensions of cognition. It would concern itself with the interpersonal and institutional processes that affect the creation, transmission, and reception of information, misinformation, and partial information. Like the sociology of knowledge, it would study not only organized science, but situational and institutional forces that affect the social dissemination of knowledge." (Goldman 1978, pp. 509-510, footnote 1). *Epistemology and Cognition* contains a larger number of passages, albeit scattered, devoted to social epistemology. (See Goldman 1986, pp. 1, 5-6, 7-8, 136-138.)

[2]   Schmitt's recollection is slightly different. He does not recall a particular course he took that covered anything on social epistemology, but he does recall encountering my ideas of the time being discussed at Michigan. He writes: "There is no doubt about one thing: I had little if any notion of social epistemology until your idea of it became fairly public information at Michigan. That would have been in my fourth year at Michigan. There was certainly a lot of discussion at Michigan of your understanding of the field of epistemology, of epistemics, and of social epistemology while I was still there" (personal communication).

mology. Schmitt later edited the first volume of new papers — again, from a classical or analytic perspective — on the theme of socializing epistemology (Schmitt 1994). My first full paper on social epistemology, "Foundations of Social Epistemics," was published in the 1987 Synthese journal issue. It explored alternative conceptualizations of the field and embraced a truth-oriented approach as the best one.

Pre-1999 Articles. "Foundations of Social Epistemics" (Goldman 1987) began by distinguishing descriptive and evaluative approaches to social epistemology (henceforth: SE). Sociologists of science were concerned with the former, but an evaluative approach, I argued, was more in line with classical epistemology. Four possible types of evaluative approach were sketched: (i) relativism, (ii) consensualism, (iii) expertism, and (iv) truth-based — or "veritistic" — evaluation. The first three options, I contended, have serious limitations, and many have little in common with classical epistemology. A veritistic mode of evaluation, by contrast, would be an excellent fit with the tradition. Finally, I saw that the broad conception of SE being charted would intersect with many empirical and policy sciences, so SE would be a multidisciplinary enterprise. I was comfortable with this, since it was in sync with the cross-disciplinary approach to individual epistemology presented in *Epistemology and Cognition* (Goldman 1986). *Epistemology and Cognition* focused on truth-linked evaluation of belief-forming processes understood as psychological processes in the cognizer's mind-brain. The natural analogue of belief-forming processes in SE would be *social practices* or *institutions*. Of course, this branch of epistemology would not be a purely descriptive science. It would assess social methods or organizational designs in terms of their intellectual "fruits", the principal fruit in the epistemic context being the learning of new truths or the uncovering of errors.

For the next dozen years my SE publications consisted of assorted articles. The themes of four of these are sketched below, grouped under three headings. The first heading is "Legal Adjudication and SE." Legal adjudication systems are frameworks within which relevant evidence is gathered and presented in court to an (individual or collective) fact-finder, which deliberates over the evidence and arrives at a judgment. Assessing the epistemic performance of such a system is a plausible valuational task for SE. An interesting aspect of the American legal adjudication system is the existence of "exclusionary" rules that allow (or require) judges to exclude evidence from court even when that evidence is relevant and reliable. Judicial exclusion of evidence looks like *paternalism*, because judges are supposed to "protect" the epistemic "interest" of fact-finders by not letting them hear evidence that would mislead them. In other sectors of social life, paternalism is often frowned upon. Should it, then, really be mandated by the law? And do exclusionary rules really promote epistemic ends? This material (and related topics) appeared in "Epistemic Paternalism: Communication Control in Law and Society" (Goldman 1991).

Another topic in the evidence territory is the so-called "discovery" rules of the Federal Rules of Civil Procedure. These rules are based on the philosophy that "prior to trial every party to a civil action is entitled to the disclosure [to the opposing party] of all relevant information in the possession of any person, unless the information is privileged." [3] Unfortunately, this principle is not always conformed to. The biggest problem concerns so-called *known negative evidence*, that is, evidence a party is aware of that tends to rebut or undermine its *own* position, and thus which it would not want to be introduced at trial. Under the adversarial system of trial procedure the parties' respective counsels are in charge of both gathering evidence and *disclosing* evidence to the opposing party, as well as arguing before the court. How well the adversary system works in motivating lawyers toward full disclosure, however, is problematic. This was explored in a paper co-authored with William Talbott, "Games Lawyers Play: Legal Discovery and Social Epistemology" (Talbott and Goldman 1998), which won the Fred Berger Prize of the American Philosophical Association in 2001.

The second heading is "Argumentation and SE". Argumentation is not simply the study of formal or informal logic. At a minimum, it is an act of assertion directed to an audience and supported by asserted premises. Or it is a sequence of such communicative acts by one speaker followed by responses by interlocutors who attempt to rebut the conclusions of earlier ones. This becomes a social epistemological matter to the extent that such acts are appraised in terms of some kind of epistemic end or desideratum, which might be to help others to get new truths or help others acquire new justified beliefs. Such an *epistemological* approach was presented in "Argumentation and Social Epistemology" (Goldman 1994) and related papers.

A third heading concerns the use of economic or quasi-economic modes of analysis in application to issues in social epistemology. One such issue is the freedom of speech. A historically influential argument for free speech has a distinctly social-epistemological flavor. It claims that freedom of speech is the best public communication system for encou-

---

[3]   Charles Alan Wright, *The Law of Federal Courts* (4th edition), p. 540 (1983).

raging a society's discovery and dissemination of the truth. The truth argument was rendered in terms of economic markets by the Supreme Court Justice Holmes, who wrote: "the ultimate good desired is better reached by free trade in ideas—...the best test of truth is the power of the thought to get itself accepted in the competition of the market..." (*Abrams v. United States*). Is this claim really supported by an economic theory of the market? James Cox and I explored this oft-repeated thesis and argued against it (Goldman and Cox 1996).

1999 Monograph. Building on these and other papers of the 1990s, I finally completed and published my long-planned monograph on social epistemology, *Knowledge in a Social World* (Goldman 1999). It began with rebuttals of standard critiques of truth-based epistemology found in the writings of social constructivists, relativists, and postmodernists. Their "veriphobia," as I characterized it, is ill-motivated. The positive challenge, however, was to build a systematic truth-oriented SE. The principal move can be expressed via a quantitative measure proposed for truth-based value. If P is a true proposition, the best doxastic attitude toward it is belief, the second best is agnosticism, and the worst is rejection.[4] At least this holds in a categorical approach to belief states. If degrees of belief, or credences, are used instead, then the higher one's credence in P the greater one's "veritistic value" (V-value) vis-à-vis P. Expressing everything in the unit interval, the categorical approach would assign $V(\text{bel } P) = 1$, $V(\text{agn } P) = .5$, and $V(\text{rej } P) = 0$. The credence approach would assign $V(\text{cred}(P) = n) = n$ (where $0 \leq n \leq 1.0$). The notion of a group's veritistic success is now readily expressible as simply the average of its members' V-values with respect to P, and changes in a group's V-value can be expressed by increases or decreases (over time) in average V-value. Next, the *extrinsic* V-value of a social practice, policy, or institutional arrangement can be captured by the extent to which it improves or reduces the community's V-values with respect to propositions of interest. Finally, if practice Π would produce greater community V-value than alternative practice Π', then Π is veritistically superior to Π'.[5]

---

4   *Knowledge in a Social World* endorsed the idea that there is a *weak* sense of 'knowledge' in which it means simply "true belief." The term "knowledge" in the title refers to this weak species of knowledge. Later I offered more detailed defense of the claim that this weak sense occurs in ordinary language (see Goldman and Olsson 2009). This is not to deny that there is also a strong sense of 'knowledge', which post-Gettier epistemologists rightfully pursue. The weak sense served better, however, for the constructive purposes of KSW, because it did not get entangled in the many disputes about a justification condition and some sort of fourth, anti-Gettierization condition.

5   My epistemic scoring scheme in KSW has been criticized by a number of writers

Various tweakings of this simple scheme are possible. For example, in certain problems selected people's veritistic success may be more important than other people's success. In a judicial context, for example, it is more important that jurors have high V-value on the core questions than an average person in the street. So those are the agents' whose veritistic status should be most heavily weighted. Separately, veritistic value is hardly the only kind of value there is. And it can be trumped by other kinds of values (e.g., moral values). So although the veritistic character of a social institution might be one evaluative dimension on which to assess such an institution, it isn't necessarily the most important one. Nor does V-value exhaust the kinds of *epistemic* value. As I emphasized in later writing, SE in general should not be wedded to veritistic value only. Justification and rationality, for example, are other species of epistemic value with which SE can be conducted.

In KSW, however, I stuck with the veritistic criterion of epistemic value, and examined a wide range of social practices and institutions in terms of it: testimony, argumentation, technologies of communication, institutions of communication, science , law, democracy, and education. Some chapters were expanded versions of papers discussed above. Here I comment on just two chapters.

Virtually all systems of legal adjudication aim at accuracy as a primary end, or at least proclaim this as an end. But how good are they, actually? Attention was focused on the two principal Europe frameworks, one of which is also found in former English colonies (including the United States). The Continental tradition, derived from ancient Roman law, employs a court in which the key players are all professional judges. They gather evidence, control the proceeding, and render a verdict. The common-law system, originating in England, has judges play a more passive role, while attorneys unearth evidence and drive the proceedings (subject to the judge's approval). A lay jury often is the finder of fact. Which system is veritistically better (and why)? Is the adversarial system better at uncovering truth because each side is a "specialist" in advocating its merits and a neutral party decides the

because it isn't a proper scoring rule. Fallis (2002) was the first to point this out; Kopec (2012) raises problems for the theory as applied to credences. He also offers a modification of the framework that carries an interesting consequence, namely, that any group whose members disagree can become more accurate by forming a consensus through averaging their credences. Olsson (2011) has an interesting theoretical discussion of a problem posed in KSW: whether veritistic SE is really an executable project. Olsson proposes a computer-simulation approach as part of the answer to this question.

matter? But might lay juries be too easily fooled by slick presentation or other misleading factors?

The most original chapter in the book (chapter 10) presents a novel analysis of the role of knowledge and ignorance in influencing the effects of democracy. Universal suffrage is commonly regarded as a touchstone of democracy. But the opportunity to cast a ballot does little good if a citizen cannot correctly identify which candidate would be more conducive to the satisfaction of his/her preferences. But if many citizens believe the true answers to their "core questions" (viz., "Which candidate would be better for me according to my lights"?), this will raise the probability of a democratically good outcome (specified in a certain way). In this fashion, knowledge possession matters crucially to democracy.

Selected Post-2000 Contributions. The central problem of SE, arguably, is the problem of testimony. When is a person justified in believing somebody's testimony, or assertion, and why? And when does testimony-based belief constitute knowledge (in the strong sense)? I have made no novel contributions to this topic in its basic form, but one of the SE papers I most enjoyed writing addresses a spin-off of this question. Suppose you are pretty uninformed on a given subject and seek advice from putative experts. They offer their opinions, but they disagree with one another. Which expert should you trust? How can a layperson even begin to weigh the comparative trustworthiness of self-proclaimed experts when he is professedly ignorant in the field? The paper spells out in worrisome detail why this is a genuinely difficult problem by virtue of the inquirer's rudimentary starting point. It then argues, however, that total skepticism is not warranted, because even if experts often consult esoteric evidence, non-esoteric evidence is sometimes available to laypersons (see Goldman 2001).

Another project I have undertaken is to propose a taxonomy, or organization, of the field of SE as a whole. This task is undertaken in two papers (Goldman 2010a, 2010b), but I focus on the first of these, originally called "Systems-Oriented Social Epistemology" and subsequently reprinted under the title "A Guide to Social Epistemology." The proposal is to divide SE into three branches, which I here label (1) *interpersonal* SE, (2) *collective* SE, and (3) *institutional* SE. Interpersonal SE concentrates on individual agents in their guise as doxastic decision-makers. What makes this *social* epistemology is the doxastic agent's use of *social evidence,* i.e., evidence concerning the speech acts or belief states of other people. So understood, the interpersonal branch of SE subsumes two of the most popular topics in current SE: the problems of testimony-based belief and peer disagreement.

Collective SE concentrates on *group* epistemic agents, such as commissions, committees, teams, courts of law, and the like. As many philosophers emphasize, we ordinarily ascribe propositional attitudes — including beliefs — to groups or collectivities of various sorts. If these "plural" entities qualify as believers, why not as knowers, as rational creatures, and so forth? This perspective is adopted within the collective branch of SE.

Institutional SE concentrates on social systems or institutions of various sorts, characterized by rules, procedures, networks of communication and influence, and so forth. Within this wing of SE, such systems or institutions are not conceived of as epistemic agents in themselves. But they have characteristics that influence and shape epistemic activities that occur within them, e.g., the conduct of trials, the peer review mechanism of science, and its reward system for scientific discoveries. Any and all of these institutional properties can influence epistemic outcomes.

3. What is the proper role of social epistemology in relation to other disciplines?

I make no secret of my view that SE should be an interdisciplinary subject. True, there are certain problems of SE that are philosophical through and through, where it is hard to imagine essential inputs from other disciplines. Peer disagreement is a good example. Other topics in SE, however, especially those in the second and third branches of SE, clearly invite inputs from particular empirical disciplines and public policy-related fields.

Social relationships and outcomes depend heavily on informational states of the participants. So it is inevitable that practitioners who work in relevant fields, and study them as academics, are often driven to discuss the role of knowledge in their fields. When they do this, they are pursuing SE at least at a rudimentary level. In short, people primarily affiliated with field X (distinct from philosophy) might wind up doing work that substantially *intersects* with what philosophers-of-X do when they approach X from an informational perspective.

There are two kinds of intersections worth distinguishing. In one kind of intersection, there is no fundamental difference between the character of the work done by philosophers and non-philosophers. Consider, for example, *social network theory,* a bundle of theoretical tools for addressing dynamic relations among groups of participants (see Easley and Kleinberg 2010). Non-philosophers might apply it to their own local domain, e.g., economic markets, the world-wide web, or epidemics. Epistemologists apply variants of it to dynamic epistemic interactions among groups of individuals.

Another type of case is where an empirical social scientist identifies an existing inquiry-motivating component in the social system of science and studies it descriptively. A philosopher then comes along and asks normative questions about it: is it an optimal device for promoting epistemic ends? A perfect example is the priority rule in science, in which all the reward for a given discovery is conferred on the first discoverer. This scheme was first pinpointed and described by the sociologist Robert Merton; then the philosophers Philip Kitcher (1990) and Michael Strevens (2003) came along to analyze the mechanism from an epistemic-evaluative perspective.

Given what has been said already, it would hardly be a surprise to find that SE contributors to a given topic may hold appointments in different disciplines although they do rather similar work. This pattern is found in many special issues of the journal *Episteme* (which concentrates on social epistemology). These journal issues include "Diversity and Dissent" (*Episteme* 3(3), 2006); "Epistemic Approaches to Democracy" (*Episteme* 5(1), 2008); "Evidence and Law" (*Episteme* 5(3), 2008); "The Epistemology of Mass Collaboration" (*Episteme* 6(1), 2009); "Computer Simulations of Social Epistemology" (*Episteme* 6(2), 2009); and "Interactive Epistemology" (*Episteme* 8(3), 2011). In addition, several of the authors in these issues were originally trained in philosophy but now hold appointments (or partial appointments) in other SE-related disciplines or fields of endeavor, e.g., Susan Haack, Larry Laudan, and Edward Stein in law; Christian List and Philip Pettit in political science; Don Fallis and Luciano Floridi in information science; and Lawrence Sanger, co-founder of *Wikipedia.*

4. What have been the most significant advances in social epistemology?

Sticking mainly to informal SE (the part I know best), it is pretty obvious that testimony and peer disagreement are the two most discussed topics. And there is little reason to doubt that they have seen the most significant advances. Testimony is the most intensively debated topic, with influential monographs and articles by C.A.J. Coady, Elizabeth Fricker, Tyler Burge, Jennifer Lackey, Sanford Goldberg, Richard Moran, and Michael Welbourne, as well as an anthology edited by Jennifer Lackey and Ernest Sosa. Similarly, the problem of peer disagreement has featured important papers by Richard Feldman, David Christensen, Adam Elga, Thomas Kelly, and Roger White, as well as an important anthology edited by Feldman and Warfield. A general anthology of social epistemology, co-edited by Alvin Goldman and Dennis Whitcomb, devotes fully two-fifths of its contents to these two topics. Similarly, eight of fifteen papers in a collection of SE papers edited by Adrian Haddock, Alan Millar and Duncan Pritchard are devoted to testimony and two other papers to disagreement. Thus, two-thirds of that volume is devoted to these two topics.

The most significant advances in formal SE, by my lights, have been the emergence of computer simulations of SE and the work on judgment aggregation. I leave a fuller discussion of computer simulation to other contributors to the present volume. The subject of judgment aggregation has been spear-headed by Christian List, Philip Pettit, and Franz Dietrich.

5. What are the most important open problems in social epistemology and what are the prospects for progress?

In philosophy everything is open, all of the time; ditto for social epistemology.

References

Easley, David and Kleinberg, Jon (2010). *Networks, Crowds, and Markets*. Cambridge: Cambridge University Press.

Fallis, Don (2002). "Goldman on Probabilistic Inference," *Philosophical Studies* 109(3): 223 240.

Goldman, Alvin
  (1967). "A Causal Theory of Knowing," *Journal of Philosophy* 64(12): 357-372

  (1976). "Discrimination and Perceptual Knowledge," *Journal of Philosophy* 73: 771-791.

  (1978). "Epistemics: The Regulative Theory of Cognition," *Journal of Philosophy* 75(10): 509-523.

  (1979). "What Is Justified Belief?" In G. Pappas, ed., *Justification and Knowledge*.

  (1986). *Epistemology and Cognition*. Cambridge, Mass: Harvard University Press.

(1987). "Foundations of Social Epistemics," *Synthese* 73(1): 109-144.

(1991). "Epistemic Paternalism: Communication Control in Law and Society," *Journal of Philosophy* 88: 113-131.

(1994). "Argumentation and Social Epistemology," *Journal of Philosophy* 91: 27-49.

(1999). *Knowledge in a Social World*. Oxford: Oxford University Press.

(2001). "Experts: Which Ones Should You Trust?" *Philosophy and Phenomenological Research* 63(1): 85-110.

(2010a). "Systems-Oriented Social Epistemology," in T. Gendler and J. Hawthorne (eds.), *Oxford Studies in Epistemology,* vol. 3, pp. 189-214, Oxford: Oxford University Press. Reprinted under the title "A Guide to Social Epistemology" in Goldman and Whitcomb (2010) and Goldman (2012).

(2010b). "Is Social Epistemology *Real* Epistemology?" In Haddock, A., Millar, A. and Pritchard, D. (eds.), *Social Epistemology*. Oxford: Oxford University Press. Reprinted in Goldman (2012).

(2012). *Reliabilism and Contemporary Epistemology: Essays*. New York: Oxford University Press.

Goldman, Alvin I. and Cox, James (1996). "Speech, Truth, and the Free Market for Ideas," *Legal Theory* 2: 1-32.

Goldman, Alvin I. and Olsson, Erik J. (2009). "Reliabilism and the Value of Knowledge," in Haddock, A., Millar, A., and Pritchard, D., eds., *Epistemic Value*. Oxford: Oxford University Press.

Goldman, Alvin I. and Whitcomb, Dennis (eds.) (2011). *Social Epistemology: Essential Readings*. New York: Oxford University Press.

Kitcher, Philip (1990). "The Division of Cognitive Labor," *Journal of Philosophy* 87: 5-21.

Kopec, Matthew (2012). "We Ought to Agree: A Consequence of Repairing Goldman's Group Scoring Rule," *Episteme* 9(2): 101-114.

Kuhn, Thomas (1962). *The Structure of Scientific Revolutions*. Chicago, IL: University of Chicago Press.

Olsson, Erik J. (2011). "A Simulation Approach to Veritistic Social Epistemology," *Episteme* 8(2): 127-143.

Rorty, Richard (1979). *Philosophy and the Mirror of Nature*. Princeton: Princeton University Press.

Schmitt, Frederick F., issue editor (1987). "Social Epistemology," *Synthese* 73(1): 1-204.

Schmitt, Frederick F., editor (1994). *Socializing Epistemology: The Social Dimensions of Knowledge*. Lanham, MD: Roman and Littlefield.

Strevens, Michael (2003). "The Role of the Priority Rule in Science," *Journal of Philosophy* 100: 55-79.

Talbott, William J. and Goldman, Alvin I. (1998). "Games Lawyers Play: Legal Discovery and Social Epistemology," *Legal Theory* 4(2): 93-163.

Wright, Charles Alan (1983). *The Law of Federal Courts* , 4th edition.

10

Philip Kitcher

John Dewey Professor of Philosophy
Columbia University

---

1. Why were you initially drawn to social epistemology?

I came to social epistemology without knowing that that was what I was approaching – and perhaps, given the idiosyncrasies of my own conception of social epistemology, it will turn out that 'social epistemology' is the wrong designation for the target. Throughout my career, I have been concerned with the possibility of integrating an understanding of the objectivity of our best forms of knowledge – realized in many parts of the social sciences, but also, with equal excellence, in areas of the humanities and social sciences – with the insights obtained from the history and sociology of science. For the past fifty years, ever since the publication of Kuhn's influential monograph, *The Structure of Scientific Revolutions*, philosophers of science have faced the challenge of replacing the over-simple models devised by the logical empiricists so that they can account better for the complexities of scientific decision-making and scientific progress. The social emphasis of Kuhn's work, greatly amplified by some of the scholars whom he influenced (including many he viewed as misunderstanding his central ideas), led me to think about the growth of knowledge in different ways, and that shift was intensified by my own investigations of aspects of the history and sociology of particular sciences. The idea of representing the growth of knowledge by specifying the probabilities assigned to a set of statements by a single agent, who then uses some rule to update them in light of the evidence, came to appear absurd to me: not only for the familiar reasons that the probabilities are typically not well-defined, that the body of evidence available is typically inconsistent, and that sorting it out and using it in evaluating hypotheses often requires forms of judgment we don't yet know how to formalize, but also because inquiry is a collective process, involving people with different points of view. Out of all this came a focus on a particular problem: is diversity valuable for scientific communities, and, if so, how is it sustained?

Since I was interested in the models used in parts of evolutionary biology and in parts of economics, that led quite quickly to the exploration
of formal models of scientific communities under particular conditions.
If I have done any social epistemology, that's probably a part of what
I've done in it. But, as I started to investigate a particular program of
scientific research, the nascent Human Genome Project, and to consider its implications for a range of social questions, I began to conceive
social epistemology in a broader sense.

Specifically, I started to move away from the terms in which I had previously looked for a historically and socially sensitive account of the
objectivity of the sciences, focused on defending the power of research
to deliver truth, to fashion reliable methods, and to make progress. I
came to view Science (capitalized!) as an institution with an important
social role. Long before I explicitly thought of myself as a pragmatist,
I saw epistemology and philosophy of science as primarily directed
towards making inquiry go better (see Kitcher 1992, for example). I
had little patience with the thought that these subjects were primarily
concerned with the analysis of 'S knows that p', or with arcane disputes about foundationalism or hoary versions of skepticism; (the exciting thing about the challenges from history and sociology of science
was that they seemed to pose *live* forms of skepticism). But, during the
1990s and thereafter, I gravitated from thinking of truth as a fundamental value to viewing it as something that is instrumental to even deeper
ends. I became concerned with neglected issues in the politics of the
sciences, and with the ways that Science might be integrated with democratic values. So I would now campaign for a far richer conception
of social epistemology than the one of my formal modeling days in the
early 1990s.

It may be worth relating my coming to social epistemology to the
work of three prominent contributors. Although I was grateful for C.A.
Coady's book on testimony, because it revived philosophical interest in
the social dimensions of knowledge, it has always seemed to me that
the epistemological reaction to it has been far too conservative: "now
we can do even more analytic epistemology with even more bells and
whistles!" Quite early on in my attempts to model scientific communities, I was encouraged by some convergence between my own ideas
and those of Alvin Goldman, although I now see Alvin as advocating
a perspective on the field that contains only a part of what should have
been there. More and more, since I first read her pioneering *Science
as Social Knowledge*, I have found the ideas of Helen Longino to be
deep and important, and, for all the disagreements we have had along

the way, I would now view her as anticipating by years many of the perspectives towards which I have struggled. If I had learned from her earlier (and I didn't lack for opportunities) I'd have spared myself considerable trouble.

2. What are your main contributions to the field of social epistemology?

I hope that (Kitcher 1990, and Kitcher 1993 chapter 8) display a style of thinking about collective inquiry. These writings show how considerations that epistemologists typically exclude from their accounts can play a positive role in the growth of knowledge. They attempt to provide a mathematical treatment of problems about the diversity of views within scientific communities and about reliance on the authority of others. So I ask, with respect to a particular type of research context, what distribution of effort would maximize the community's chance of success. Since that turns out often to be different from what individual agents working in an uncoordinated fashion would do, it leads to the question of how their endeavors might be coordinated to produce a good division of labor. I show that the competition for credit can play a positive role. Effectively, if scientists are motivated by "grubby" goals (wanting to win big prizes), the community research might go better than if they are impeccably rational.

Whether these are the only styles of models we need, whether they fall victim to the sorts of critiques often made of economic and ecological models, and whether a serious analysis of any facet of community organization needs to be considered in the light of all its effects on the processes of collective investigation all seem to me to be important questions. Yet even if they were answered in ways unfavorable to the analyses I offered, I continue to believe that my preliminary analyses would be valuable in their stimulus to overcome the deficiencies and do better.

The more qualitative work I have done recently, investigating the ways in which particular areas of research integrate with the values and goals of societies seems to me to point towards a renewal of the philosophy of science. Just as analytic epistemology has become bogged down on a few tiny topics of concern only to a handful of (obsessive?) specialists, so too, the general philosophy of science has largely run out of steam. It appears evident to me that the principal methodological accomplishments of the past decades have been the formulation by Clark Glymour and his colleagues, and by Judea Pearl, of techniques for arriving at causal conclusions from statistical data, as well as the new perspectives offered by Nancy Cartwright and the many people who have been influenced by her. Pretty much everything else that *ge-*

neral philosophy of science has done has been irrelevant to scientific practice. That is decidedly not true, however, of the wealth of subtle and informed work carried out in the philosophy of the special sciences – not only in philosophy of physics, but in the philosophy of biology, of archeology, of economics, and, increasingly, of chemistry and of the sciences of complex systems.

The biggest gap has been the general study of science as a community project, where there is much to be said. I hope that my own work, particularly (Kitcher 2001, Kitcher 2011a), as well as classic studies by Helen Longino, can help prepare the way for this.

3. What is the proper role of social epistemology in relation to other disciplines?

As I see it, the main task of social epistemology is to pose, and address, questions about the organization of inquiry, understood as a collective endeavor, aimed at the promotion of collective well-being. Hence, the first normative task is to understand how to think about collective well-being, and this is where my ideal of well-ordered science makes its appearance. Roughly, inquiry should be organized to do as well as it can in advancing the projects people identify as central to their lives. Since it's evident that it's very hard to make everyone's ventures go wonderfully well, there have to be trade-offs: the ideal discussion central to well-ordered science provides a way of working out how that might be done. It now seems to me important to recognize that values come in right away in thinking about Science – we should give up the old, bashful practice of mumbling a bit about "science and values" at the ends of books or courses, and confront the issue of value-judgments up front. (I pursue this stance in Kitcher 2011a, and try to work out the background perspective in some detail in Kitcher 2011b).

Science, or inquiry generally, is in the business of delivering information that is directed towards the right questions, that is true enough to meet the purposes lying behind those questions, that is reliable enough for those who pose them, and is accessible to those who need it. All these pragmatic notions get their content from the ideal of well-ordered science. So, first of all, there's a value-theoretic bit. Beyond that, if you want to provide a critique or appraisal of current ways of organizing inquiry, or of alternatives we might substitute for them, all sorts of disciplines are likely to be pertinent. Social and political theory are needed to understand the ways in which Science interacts with other institutions to bear on human well-being. Economics is often profoundly pertinent to these assessments. Historical and sociological studies of particular episodes of research can be profoundly illuminating, offering us a range of cases for comparison, as well as useful conceptual tools. In the end, it would be good to devise precise analyses of various modes of organization – highly-developed versions of the models I originally tried to work out – and in doing this it's important not only to make use of existing formal methods and techniques, but to consider possibilities of expanding our repertoire (here Glymour and Pearl have shown both the potential and the amount of labor that is needed).

I think of social epistemology as a highly multidisciplinary subject. Perhaps it is so richly interdisciplinary that philosophers should form parts of teams, alongside natural scientists, sociologists, economists, political theorists, historians and maybe others.

4. What have been the most significant advances in social epistemology?

One of the most obvious major contributions is the field-defining book by Alvin Goldman (1999), followed up by his dedicated founding and editing of *Episteme*. A great merit of the book is its wide ranging over various domains in which investigations are carried out, together with its characteristically careful and lucid formulation of the "veritistic" approach. Goldman's synthesis allows his successors to pose many good questions in social epistemology, and much of its influence has been benign. My only reservations are that its scope seems to me to exclude parts of the more general way of thinking about inquiry I prefer, and that its emphasis on analytic tasks can easily divert philosophy from its proper – meliorative – project, towards the activity of "reflecting on our social epistemological practices and trying to make sense of them", an activity that can, all too easily, settle into those recondite and isolated ventures in "intuition-trading" that people engaged in serious inquiry find so perplexing (and often ludicrous). Nevertheless, this is a major step forward in defining an important, neglected, and embryonic area of philosophy.

A second large achievement is the use of sophisticated modeling to understand the ways in which beliefs flow through communities by processes of social contagion. Rainer Hegselmann and his collaborators have produced illuminating studies in this area, even though, as far as I can tell, their work is almost unknown to many social epistemologists (including many who would benefit from it).

A third important line of work – although here my own fondness for my efforts of the early 1990s may mislead me – is the sequence of formal studies undertaken by younger scholars who have thought about aspects of the dynamics of research in scientific communities. I have in mind Michael Strevens' excellent paper on the priority rule, as well as more recent essays by Michael Weisberg, Kevin Zollman, and Ryan Muldoon.

Finally, Helen Longino's *Science as Social Knowledge* strikes me as outstandingly important. It has raised a large number of new questions about scientific inquiry. My own efforts at understanding Science as a social institution within democratic societies come at some of the same issues from a different angle (Kitcher 2001, 2011a), but Longino deserves the credit for charting the way.

5. What are the most important open problems in social epistemology and what are the prospects for progress?

The big question seems to me to be: "How should collective inquiry be organized?" I think of this as the social analogue of the driving question for individualistic epistemology, the question that inspired Descartes to write the *Regulae*, the *Discourse on Method*, and the *Meditations*. The major open problems derive from the big question.

Some of them are normative. We need a clear account of what the goals of inquiry are. This leads, I believe, into issues about how to understand the notion of a significant question (the territory I've tried to explore in my discussions of well-ordered science [Kitcher 2001, 2011a]). Armed with an account of goals, you can then start to examine various features of inquiry as it now exists, and try to see if it's well-adapted to delivering those goals.

Here are a few issues that might then come up. (1) How do you find your way to reliable information in a world awash with potential sources? (2) Do contemporary communities of inquirers have enough diversity of opinion? (3) Are some structures that currently exist (for example, the priority rule for awarding credit) conducive to various desirable types of cooperation (sharing partial results, say)? (4) How should scientific research be integrated into the economic framework we have (or, possibly, how should that economic framework itself be modified so that scientific research can go well)? (5) What standards of certification of public knowledge are appropriate for societies within which there are radically incompatible attitudes towards different texts and traditions? These are the sorts of questions I'd particularly like to see answered, but there are many others that can be generated from the big question.

Progress in answering them will almost certainly depend on how education in philosophy goes. If students are trained so that their reading is confined to the professional journals, and if they think they should spend their lives trading intuitions about ever more fanciful cases, the prospects for philosophical progress in any area are pretty grim. Social epistemology should require philosophers to go out and learn a lot of things: as I've emphasized, all sorts of disciplines are relevant. I hope enough young people will find social epistemology exciting, challenging, and relevant, so that they expand their areas of competence and fulfill the promise of the field.

Bibliography

Kitcher, Philip 1990 "The Division of Cognitive Labor", *Journal of Philosophy*, 87, 5-22

Kitcher, Philip 1992 "The Naturalists Return", *Philosophical Review*, 101, 53-114

Kitcher, Philip 1993 *The Advancement of Science*, New York: Oxford University Press

Kitcher, Philip 2001 *Science, Truth, and Democracy*, New York: Oxford University Press

Kitcher, Philip 2011a *Science in a Democratic Society*, Amherst NY: Prometheus Books

Kitcher, Philip 2011b *The Ethical Project*, Cambridge MA: Harvard University Press

11

Martin Kusch

Professor for Philosophy of Science and Epistemology
University of Vienna, Austria

1. Why were you initially drawn to social epistemology?

This is the second time that I have the honor of contributing to this series: I also wrote an entry for the volume on epistemology (Kusch 2008). Since it seems desirable for both contributions to be intelligible on their own, a certain amount of overlap between my two sets of answers is unavoidable.

"Social epistemology" (SE) can be understood broadly or narrowly. On the broad understanding, the expression covers all systematic reflection on the social nature or dimensions of cognitive achievements such as knowledge, true belief, justified belief, understanding, or wisdom. The sociology of knowledge, the social history of science, or the philosophy of the social sciences are amongst the key parts of SE thus construed. Many contributors to Pragmatism, Marxism, Critical Theory or Hermeneutics also qualify. On the narrow understanding, SE dates from the 1980s, is primarily a philosophical enterprise, and has its roots in Anglo-American epistemology, in feminist theory, as well as in the philosophy of science.

It is only against the background of the broad conception of SE that I am able to explain how I first got drawn into the field and why my preoccupation with it has not lessened. My interest in SE was first triggered by work in the so-called "Continental Tradition" and by *historical* and *social-political* questions about *scientific* knowledge.

Although I am German by origin, for personal reasons I studied in Finnish universities (1981 to 1989), first in Jyväskylä, later in Helsinki and Oulu. The Jyväskylä department encouraged interest in German-speaking philosophy. Accordingly, the first authors who captured my philosophical imagination were Hegel, Husserl, Heidegger, Gadamer and Habermas. I did not specifically focus on epistemological issues during my pre-PhD days, though I recall studying Hegel's critique of the Kantian project of epistemology as first philosophy, Husserl's heroic struggles with epistemological relativism, Heidegger's criticism of

Husserl's foundationalism, or Habermas' attempt to analyze (scientific) knowledge in terms of social interests.

I became fascinated with SE (broadly construed) only after the completion of my PhD thesis (on philosophy of language in Husserl and Heidegger, supervised by Jaakko Hintikka). In 1988 the University of Oulu was looking for a temporary replacement to teach history of ideas, and I got the job. The history students were not interested in "incomprehensible German philosophers starting with the letter 'H'" (as my friend Calvin Normore once jokingly put it), and they asked me to lecture instead on new Anglo-American and French ideas in the history, philosophy and sociology of science. This demand lead me to study the work of Michel Foucault, the French tradition of "epistémologie" (Gaston Bachelard, Georges Canguilhem), and the "Sociology of Scientific Knowledge" (especially David Bloor, Barry Barnes, Harry Collins, Simon Schaffer and Steve Shapin). I do not know whether the Oulu students got much out of my lectures on these authors, but I was hooked. The eventual results were books on Foucault's historiography (1991) and on the sociology of knowledge (1995, 1998, 1999). And in 1992 I was hired by the famous Science Studies Unit of the University of Edinburgh.

For a while—between 1991 and 1996—I identified more with history and sociology than with any part of philosophy. Nevertheless I always thought, or hoped, that my primary audience would be philosophers. My social histories of the politics of classic controversies in the history of German-speaking philosophy of the early twentieth century—be it over naturalism, be it over the nature of thought—were meant to deepen and widen philosophers' own reflections concerning the determinants, structures and closure mechanisms of philosophical disputes. For me such issues were, and are, central to SE.

My interest in SE *narrowly conceived* emerged in 1997 when I took up a permanent position in the Department of History and Philosophy of Science at the University of Cambridge. I was hired as a philosopher of science. In our first chat my new head of department, Peter Lipton, expressed the hope that I would "turn to more philosophical-epistemological work". This chat was the beginning of a ten-year-long philosophical conversation between us, much of which focused on SE, and especially on testimony. (It lasted until Peter's premature death in 2007.) A jointly edited volume on testimony in the sciences was the most tangible outcome (Kusch and Lipton 2002). I also learnt much from other Cambridge epistemologists (both widely and narrowly construed). I only had a few brief conversations with Edward Craig when I first arrived in Cambridge, but his book *Knowledge and the State of Nature* (1990) impressed me greatly. It took me a long time to develop the courage to push Craig's line of investigation further.

Almost equally important in stimulating my interest in SE (narrowly conceived) was Alvin Goldman's *Knowledge in a Social World* (1999). I still admire Goldman's ability to bring social-epistemological reflection to bear on a very wide range of topics, from education to philosophy of science, from law to testimony. I greatly appreciated Tony Coady's *Testimony* (1992) for the same reason. Coady's book shows why philosophical reflection on testimony matters, and matters well beyond the realm of social epistemology.

My work since the late nineties has tried to bridge the gap between the sociology of knowledge and SE (narrowly conceived). Many of these attempts have fallen between the two stools. Advocates of SE (narrowly conceived) think of the sociology of knowledge as a philosophically shallow form of epistemic relativism. And my friends in the sociology of knowledge tend to be equally dismissive of much of philosophical epistemology. Of course, I think that both assessments are flawed. Accordingly, I have sought to defend the coherence and the philosophical significance of the sociology of knowledge, including its relativism; and I have attempted to strengthen some of the "communitarian" ideas dear to sociologists of knowledge using the tools and techniques of analytic epistemology and SE.

2. What are your main contributions to the field of social epistemology?

For my work between 1991 and 2006 I can best identify these contributions by summarizing my book publications.

In my *Foucault's Strata and Fields: An Investigation into Archeological and Genealogical Science Studies* (1991), I tried to reconstruct and make plausible Foucault's historiography of science in general, and his ideas on the inseparability of scientific knowledge and social power in particular. In doing so, I related his work to sociological and anthropological science studies and to Anglo-American philosophy of science. Needless to say, much of this is now somewhat dated, but the defense of epistemological relativism that I put forward in Chapter 13 still seems right to me.

Psychologism (1995) and *Psychological Knowledge* (1999) are contributions to the "sociology of philosophical knowledge". These studies were triggered by the thought that the *history of philosophy* deserves to be written with the same kind of social-historical sensitivity which is now common in the *history of science*. Philosophers working on the history of their field usually refuse to pay much attention to the psychological, social or political factors that influenced or shaped the thinking and debates of the great philosophers of the past. Maybe it is due to my early fascination with the German philosophical tradition from Hegel to Habermas that I find this restriction to arguments and arguments alone both unhistorical and *unphilosophical*. If philosophy had an "essence", would not that essence have something to do with "reflection" and "self-awareness"? And must not this self-awareness include a serious appreciation of the historical contingency of the questions one asks and the vocabularies one employs? If philosophy is after conditions of possibility, surely the historical, social and political conditions of the possibility of philosophy itself must inevitably be a central philosophical concern (cf. Kusch 2000).

Psychologism is a sociological history of the dispute over the relationship between (experimental) psychology, epistemology and logic in German-speaking philosophy between, roughly, 1900 and 1930. I documented the wide variety of positions on this relationship, not least in order to bring out that Frege and Husserl were not lone heroic proponents of anti-psychologism. And I sought to explain the eventual (though temporary) defeat of psychologism and naturalism in social-political terms. This was meant to convince the reader that there was nothing inevitable about the (temporary) triumph of anti-psychologism, nothing inevitable about the institutional separation of psychology from the rest of philosophy, and nothing inevitable about the self-image of philosophy as based on non-empirical methods of inquiry.

The first half of *Psychological Knowledge* did something similar for the early-twentieth-century philosophical dispute in Germany over the nature of thought and the possibility of introspection (Wundt, Külpe, Müller were the key figures here). I argued that the distribution of positions was socially patterned: philosophers' stance on the nature of thought varied, amongst other things, according to their party-political and their confessional commitments. The second half of the book shifted from sociological history to "social philosophy of mind": I put forward an interpretation of folk psychology as a social institution.

The Shape of Actions: What Humans and Machines Can Do (1998) was joint work with the sociologist of scientific knowledge, Harry Collins. The book developed a social theory of the possibility of automation, with a special focus on scientific instruments. The core of our theory is a classification of actions and the various social conditions under which they can be mechanized. The theory we proposed is not a *(social) epistemology of instruments*—though perhaps a necessary prolegomenon to such epistemology.

Knowledge by Agreement: The Programme of Communitarian Epistemology (2002): When I first used the label "communitarian epistemology" I thought of it as the philosophical counterpart of the sociology of scientific knowledge, especially the relativistic "Strong Programme" advocated by Barnes and Bloor. Accordingly, *Knowledge by Agreement* tried to outline and defend—in what I hoped were recognizably philosophical ways—four epistemological theses of "Strong Programme" vintage: that our epistemic dependence upon testimony runs too deep for us to be able to produce a non-circular general justification for our trust in others' words; that testimony is a generative source of knowledge insofar as it is always in part performative; that "knower" is a social status; and that a communitarian reading of Wittgenstein supports a strong form of epistemic relativism.

There are some parts of *Knowledge by Agreement* that still seem right to me (especially Part III), but I now find the book a little too quick and programmatic for my taste. I took too much for granted, and I related to some of the sociologists' views too uncritically. I have addressed some of these shortcomings in my work of the last six years. For instance, my book *A Skeptical Guide to Meaning and Rules: Defending Kripke's Wittgenstein* (2006) defends the communitarian reading of Wittgenstein and its consequences at much greater length than anything offered in *Knowledge by Agreement*.

Over the past few years I have pursued two main social-epistemological projects that have not (yet) resulted in book-length publications. The first pushes further Edward Craig's and Bernard Williams' "state of nature epistemology". In my paper "Testimony and the Value of Knowledge" (2009c) I used their work to outline a "communitarian theory of epistemic value": at least *scientific* knowledge is valuable as a collective good. In "Knowledge and Certainties in the Epistemic State of Nature" (2011b) I conduct a critical dialogue between Craig's theory and Wittgenstein's claim—familiar from *On Certainty*—that commonsense certainties cannot be known. It turns out that Craig's distinction between different stages in the development of our concept of knowledge can illuminate and make plausible Wittgenstein's claim. But it can do so only if Craig's traditional commitment to a central "core" in our concept of knowledge is replaced with the idea of *knowledge* as a family-resemblance concept. And in "Naturalized Epistemology and the Genealogy of Knowledge" (2013) I defend and reinterpret Craig's project in response to criticism put forward by Hilary Kornblith in his recent paper "Why Should We Care about the Concept of Knowledge?" (2011). I seek to make plausible that Craig's project has affinities with naturalized epistemology, and that it helps us to understand unity and disunity in both concepts and natural kinds of knowledge.

My second current project is a book, tentatively entitled "Wittgenstein's Epistemological Investigations" (cf. Kusch 2009b, 2011a, 2011b, 2011d). Its chapters reconstruct and elaborate the various argumentative sketches of *On Certainty* by relating them to philosophical and scientific positions both of the early twentieth-century and of today. Social-epistemological themes are, unsurprisingly, paramount throughout. For instance, I argue that for Wittgenstein epistemological scepticism is committed to form of individualism, and that he inclines towards certain forms of epistemological relativism. (I have continued to evaluate arguments for and against epistemological relativism also in other places, cf. Kusch 2009a, 2010a, 2010b, 2011c).

3. What is the proper role of social epistemology in relation to other disciplines?

In answering this question I shall focus on mainstream analytical-philosophical forms of social epistemology, or SE narrowly understood. (After all, much of SE broadly construed is already part and parcel of other disciplines: anthropology, social psychology, or sociology.)

SE is obviously inseparable from epistemology itself. For instance, much of recent SE has focused on testimony. Testimony is one of the traditional "sources of knowledge", and closely intertwined with other sources such as perception, reasoning, or memory. Moreover, the same general theories of epistemic justification that have been debated concerning knowledge in general, have also been scrutinized with respect to testimony. Other disputes too—say over Timothy Williamson's "Knowledge First" thesis—have found their way from general epistemology to social epistemology.

But there is also room for dispute here: does SE build upon more traditional epistemology, or does it change its very foundations? Goldman inclines more towards the former option, I favor the latter. My main ground is that knowledge attributions are (usually) attributions of a social status. Or more generally, knowledge is a social rather than a natural kind. And that holds regardless of whether we are speaking of testimony or other sources of knowledge.

Like epistemology in general so also SE (narrowly construed) in particular has many essential links to other fields of philosophy: to the philosophy of mind (because of the concept of belief), to social ontology (because of the importance of groups), to feminism (because of the importance of political questions), or to the philosophy of science. No doubt there may be more such links that lie beyond my horizon.

Given the history of my interest in SE, it will hardly come as a surprise that I favor close interaction between SE and the sociology of (scientific) knowledge (SSK): after all, SSK is dedicated to the empirical investigation of social dimensions of knowledge. For such interaction to be possible and fruitful, social epistemologists have to get over certain stereotypes and misconceptions concerning SSK. (Cf. Kusch 2010b.)

One particularly fruitful area of collaboration between epistemologists and social scientists seems to me to be the already mentioned project of a genealogy of epistemic concepts and practices. Early chapters of genealogical narratives must inevitably be "imaginary" "just-so" stories. But other, later, chapters can be "real genealogies", that is, genealogies based on the historical record. Historical record or not, both *imaginary and real* genealogies have much to learn from anthropology, developmental psychology, and the history and sociology of science. Intriguingly enough, some leading historians of science have formed a new subfield that seems ideally suited to function as a historical counterpart to Craig's and Williams' philosophical "genealogy": the "historical epistemology" of Lorraine Daston, Peter Galison and Hans-Jörg Rheinberger. Historians of science following this programme seek to show that key epistemological concepts—like evidence, objectivity or proof—have a contingent history; that nothing about these concepts is or was inevitable or permanent.

4. What have been the most significant advances in social epistemology?

Some of the more significant advances in my view are the following:

1) The emergence and development of SSK over the past thirty years. It has given us a new understanding of the social dimension of scientific and technological work on many levels. The work of Barry Barnes, David Bloor, Harry Collins, Donald MacKenzie, Simon Schaffer and Steve Shapin must be mentioned first and foremost here.

2) The last twenty years have seen a dramatic increase in interest in the epistemology of testimony. Testimony has gone from being a neglected topic to being "where the action is". Many writers have contributed to this "revolution", but it seems fair to say that the studies by Jonathan Adler, Tyler Burge, Tony Coady, Paul Faulkner, Elizabeth and Miranda Fricker, Sandy Goldberg, John Hardwig, Jennifer Lackey, Richard Moran, Matthew Weiner, and Michael Welbourne, have been particularly and rightly influential.

3) The emergence of peer disagreement as a central topic seems to be another major development within SE of the last few years. Philosophers were always aware of testimony as a phenomenon, even when they paid little attention to it. But the peer disagreement issue seems different. It did not even feature of a list of possible topics. The pioneers here were of course David Christensen, Adam Elga, Richard Feldman, and Thomas Kelly.

4) Over the last decade many formal epistemologists have also turned their attention to social epistemology. Perhaps the most influential work has been on judgment aggregation (e.g. Christian List, Philip Pettit) and a Bayesian framework for testimony (Luc Bovens, Stephan Hartmann).

5) I also consider the coming together of political philosophy and epistemology to be a major advance. Of course feminist epistemologists (and many "Continental philosophers") have always insisted that knowledge and social power are (often? always?) intertwined if not inseparable. But the message has only slowly reached the mainstream. The success of Miranda Fricker's work—even amongst mainstream epistemologists—is a sign that things are going in the right direction.

5. What are the most important open problems in social epistemology and what are the prospects for progress?

There are a number of fronts on which I would like to see—and contribute to—more progress.

1. It has always struck me as odd that so much of twentieth-century epistemology and philosophy of science have—especially in the Anglophone world—lead separate lives. Surely social epistemology and philosophy of science would benefit from a much closer interaction. This would also lead to a closer engagement between SSK and SE. Issues on which these fields could come together include the role of testimony in the sciences, the analysis of controversy and disagreement, the study of forms of epistemic relativism and pluralism, the epistemology of instruments, or the division of cognitive labor. Some such work already exists, but so much more remains to be done.

2. Another area to which the last sentence applies might be called "collective epistemology": the study of how groups can function as epistemic agents. This area brings together "social ontology" with social epistemology. We have as yet only a poor understanding of the what is involved in trusting groups or in constructing reliable epistemic group agents.

3. I mentioned the need for political epistemology already in the last section. But I must do so again here since so many of its facets are still to be developed. I am thinking for example of the epistemology of democracy or expertise. This is one of the issues that Gold-

man identified as important back in the 1990s, and a field where social epistemology meets recent work in social studies of science (cf. the work of Harry Collins and Robert Evans).

4. The "open problem" that I myself hope to focus on is a historical and philosophical study of epistemic relativism: I want to understand historically-sociologically how epistemic relativism became—during the nineteenth century—a central topic of philosophical reflection; and I want to reply to the best of the anti-relativistic studies published by distinguished philosophers/epistemologists over the past two decades (I am thinking here especially of the books by Simon Blackburn, Paul Boghossian, Susan Haack, and Thomas Nagel).

Truth be told, I have no idea how good the chances for progress are in any of these areas. But we have got to try.

References

Adler, J. (2002), *Beliefs Own Ethics*, Cambridge, Mass.: MIT Press.

Barnes, B. (1982), T. S. *Kuhn and Social Science*, London: MacMillan.

Blackburn, S. (2005), *Truth: A Guide for the Perplexed*, London: Penguin.

Bloor, D. (1991), *Knowledge and Social Imagery*, Chicago: Chicago University Press.

Bloor, D. (1997), *Wittgenstein, Rules and Institutions*, London: Routledge.

Boghossian, P. (2006), *Fear of Knowledge: Against Relativism and Constructivism*, Oxford: Oxford University Press.

Burge, T. (1993), "Content Preservation", *The Philosophical Review* 102: 457-488.

Christensen, D. (2007), "Epistemology of Disagreement: The Good News", *Philosophical Review*, 116/2: 187-217.

Coady, C. A. J. (1992), *Testimony: A Philosophical Study*, Oxford: Oxford University Press.

Collins, H. M. (1992), *Changing Order: Replication and Induction in Scientific Practice*, 2nd ed., Chicago: University of Chicago Press.

Collins, H. M. and M. Kusch (1998), *The Shape of Actions: What Humans and Machines Can Do*, Cambridge, Mass.: MIT Press.

Collins, H. and R. Evans (2007), *Rethinking Expertise*, Chicago and London: University of Chicago Press.

Craig, E. (1990), *Knowledge and the State of Nature: An Essay in Conceptual Synthesis*, Oxford: Clarendon.

Daston, L. and P. Galison (2007), *Objectivity*, New York: Zone Books.

Elga, A. (2007), "Reflection and Disagreement", *Nous* 41: 478-502.

Faulkner, P. (2011), *Knowledge on Trust*, Oxford: Oxford University Press.

Feldman, R. (2007), "Reasonable Religious Disagreements", in L. Antony (ed.), *Philosophers without Gods: Meditations on Atheism and the Secular Life*, Oxford: Oxford University Press, 194-214.

Fricker, E. (1987), "The Epistemology of Testimony", *Proceedings of the Aristotelian Society*, supp. Vol. 61: 57-83.

Fricker, M. (2007), *Epistemic Injustice: Power & the Ethics of Knowing*, Oxford: Oxford University Press.

Goldberg, S. (2010), *Relying on Others: An Essay in Epistemology*, Oxford: Oxford University Press.

Goldman, A. (1999), *Knowledge in a Social World*, Princeton and Oxford: Oxford University Press.

Haack, S. (1998), *Confessions of a Passionate Moderate*, Chicago: Chicago University Press.

Hardwig, J. (1985), "Epistemic Dependence", *Journal of Philosophy* 82: 335-349.

Kelly, T. (2005), "The Epistemic Significance of Disagreement", in T. S. Gendler and J. Hawthorne (eds.), *Oxford Studies in Epistemology, I*, Oxford: Oxford University Press, 167-196.

Kornblith, H. (2011), "Why Should We Care about the Concept of Knowledge?" *Episteme* 8: 38-52.

Kusch, M. (1989), *Language as Calculus vs. Language as Universal Medium: A Study in Husserl, Heidegger and Gadamer*, Dordrecht: Kluwer.

Kusch, M. (1991), *Foucault's Strata and Fields: An Investigation into Archaeological and Genealogical Science Studies*, Dordrecht: Kluwer.

Kusch, M. (1995), *Psychologism: A Case Study in the Sociology of Philosophical Knowledge*, London: Routledge.

Kusch, M. (1999), *Psychological Knowledge: A Social History and Philosophy*, London: Routledge.

Kusch, M. (ed.) (2000), *The Sociology of Philosophical Knowledge*, Dordrecht: Kluwer.

Kusch, M. (2002), *Knowledge by Agreement: The Programme of Communitarian Epistemology*, Oxford: Oxford University Press.

Kusch, M. (2006), *A Sceptical Guide to Meaning and Rules: Defending Kripke's Wittgenstein*, Chesham: Acumen.

Kusch, M. (2007), "Towards a Political Philosophy of Risk: Experts and Publics in Deliberative Democracy", in T. Lewens (ed.), *Risk: Philosophical Perspectives*, London: Routledge, 131-155.

Kusch, M. (2008), Five Answers, in F. Hendricks and D. Pritchard (eds.), *Epistemology: Five Questions*, Automatic Press, 217-230.

Kusch, M. (2009a), "Epistemic Replacement Relativism Defended", in M. Suarez, M. Dorato, M. Redei (hrsg.), *EPSA Epistemology and Methodology of Science*, Berlin, New York: Springer, 165-176.

Kusch, M. (2009b), "Kripke's Wittgenstein, *On Certainty*, and Epistemic Relativism", in D. Whiting (hrsg.), *The Later Wittgenstein on Language*, Houndmills, Basingstoke: Palgrave Macmillan, 213-230.

Kusch, M. (2009c), "Testimony and the Value of Knowledge", in A. Haddock, A. Millar, and D. Pritchard (eds.), Epistemic Value, Oxford: Oxford University Press, 60-94.

Kusch, M. (2010a), "Hacking's Historical Epistemology: A Critique of Styles of Reasoning", *Studies in History and Philosophy of Science, Part A*, 41, 158-73.

Kusch, M. (2010b), "Social Epistemology", in Sven Bernecker und Duncan Pritchard (eds.), *The Routledge Companion to Epistemology*, London: Routledge, 873-884.

Kusch, M. (2011a), "Disagreement and Picture in Wittgenstein's 'Lectures on Religious Belief'", in R. Heinrich et al. (eds.), *Image and Imaging in Philosophy, Science and the Arts, Volume 1*, Frankfurt: Ontos, 35-58.

Kusch, M. (2011b), "Knowledge and Certainties in the Epistemic State of Nature", *Episteme* 8: 6-23.

Kusch, M. (2011c), "Reflexivity, Relativism, Microhistory: Three Desiderata for Historical Epistemologies", *Erkenntnis* 75: 483-494.

Kusch, M. (2011d), "Wittgenstein and Einstein's Clocks", in E. Ramharter (ed.), *Unsocial Sociabilities: Wittgenstein's Sources*, Berlin: Parerga, 203-218.

Kusch, M. (2013), "Naturalized Epistemology and the Genealogy of Knowledge", in M. Lenz and A. Waldow (eds.), Contemporary Perspectives on Early Modern Philosophy, Dordrecht: Springer, 87-97.

Kusch, M. and P. Lipton (2002), "Testimony and the Sciences", Special Volume, *Studies in History and Philosophy of Science* 33A.

Lackey, J. (2008), *Learning from Words: Testimony as a Source of Knowledge*, Oxford: Oxford University Press.

List, C. and P. Pettit (2011), *Group Agency: The Possibility, Design, and Status of Corporate Agents*, Oxford: Oxford University Press.

MacKenzie, D. (2001), *Mechanizing Proof: Computing, Risk and Trust*, Cambridge, Mass.: MIT Press.

Moran, R. (2006), "Getting Told and Being Believed", in J. Lackey and E. Sosa (eds.), *The Epistemology of Testimony*, Oxford: Oxford University Press, 272-306.

Nagel, T. (1997), *The Last Word*, Oxford: Oxford University Press.

Rheinberger, H.-J. (2007), *Historische Epistemologie*, Hamburg: Junius.

Shapin, S. (1994), *A Social History of Truth*, Chicago: University of Chicago Press.

Shapin S. and S. Schaffer (1985), *Leviathan and the Air-Pump*, Princeton, N.J.: Princeton University Press.

Weiner, M. (2003), "Accepting Testimony", *The Philosophical Quarterly* 53: 256-264.

Welbourne, M. (1986), *The Community of Knowledge*, Aberdeen: Aberdeen University Press.

Williams, B. (2002), *Truth and Truthfulness: An Essay in Genealogy*, Princeton and Oxford: Oxford University Press.

Williamson, T. (2000), *Knowledge and Its Limits*, Oxford: Oxford University Press.

12

Jennifer Lackey

Professor of Philosophy
Northwestern University

---

1. Why were you initially drawn to social epistemology?

I was initially drawn to social epistemology through an interest in testimony. Despite the fact that our reliance on the reports of others is both deep and ubiquitous, very little work in epistemology had been devoted to a sustained and systematic treatment of the topic. Moreover, the main exception to this at the time—C.A.J. Coady's 1992 book, *Testimony: A Philosophical Study*—relied on a central thesis that struck me as fundamentally incorrect; namely, that hearers can acquire testimonial knowledge only if the speakers in question possess the knowledge themselves. My goal was to develop and defend an alternative account of the epistemology of testimony that did not rely on this thesis.

2. What are your main contributions to the field of social epistemology?

My central contributions to social epistemology fall under three main topics: testimony, disagreement, and collective epistemology. With respect to the epistemology of testimony, I published a book, *Learning from Words: Testimony as a Source of Knowledge*, in which I take up the question how precisely we acquire knowledge through the testimony of others. Despite the differences found among the views answering this question, the thesis mentioned above is nearly universally accepted: knowledge is acquired through the process of *transmission* from speakers to hearers. According to this *transmission thesis*, then, hearers can acquire knowledge on the basis of the testimony of speakers only if the speakers themselves possess the knowledge in question.[1] My aim in *Learning from Words* is to show that the transmission thesis is fundamentally incorrect. In particular, I argue that hearers *can* acquire

---

[1] Proponents of this thesis include Welbourne (1979, 1981, 1986, and 1994), Hardwig (1985 and 1991), Ross (1986), Burge (1993 and 1997), Plantinga (1993), McDowell (1994), Williamson (1996 and 2000), Audi (1997, 1998, and 2006), Owens (2000 and 2006), Reynolds (2002), Faulkner (2006), and Schmitt (2006).

testimonial knowledge from speakers who do not themselves possess the knowledge in question because *unreliable knowers* may nonetheless be *reliable testifiers*. For instance, an elementary school teacher who is a devout creationist may reject all of the evidence supporting evolutionary theory, thereby failing to know that modern day *Homo sapiens* evolved from *Homo erectus*. Nevertheless, she may reliably convey this fact to her students, thereby imparting knowledge to her students that she fails to possess herself. Because of this, testimony is not merely a transmissive epistemic source but, instead, can generate new knowledge in its own right. I then develop and defend an alternative account: whereas the views dominant in the literature focus on the internal states of speakers—such as states of *knowing* and *believing*—I advance a new theory of testimony that instead focuses on the linguistic or communicative items in testimonial exchanges—such as *statements* and other *acts of communication*. The upshot of these considerations is that, strictly speaking, we do not learn from one another's states of knowing—we *learn from one another's words*. In order to make genuine progress in the epistemology of testimony, then, I argue that we need to stop looking at what speakers *know* and focus, instead, on what speakers *say*.

Once this radical shift in focus is in place, I turn to the role of the hearer in testimonial exchanges: in order to acquire justified belief from a speaker's words, is it sufficient for the hearer to merely lack defeaters, thereby rendering testimony an autonomous epistemic source—as *non-reductionists*[2] in the epistemology of testimony maintain—or must the hearer also possess positive reasons, thereby rendering testimony reducible to more basic epistemic sources—as *reductionists*[3] hold? I argue that both of these answers are inadequate: positive reasons are necessary for testimonial justification, but testimony itself is an irreducible epistemic source. This leads to the development of my *dualist* view,

---

[2]   Proponents of various versions of non-reductionism include Austin (1979), Welbourne (1979, 1981, 1986, and 1994), Evans (1982), Reid (1983), Ross (1986), Hardwig (1985 and 1991), Coady (1992 and 1994), Burge (1993 and 1997), Plantinga (1993), Webb (1993), Dummett (1994), Foley (1994), McDowell (1994), Strawson (1994), Williamson (1996 and 2000), Goldman (1999), Schmitt (1999), Owens (2000 and 2006), Rysiew (2002), Weiner (2003), Goldberg (2010), and Sosa (2006). Some phrase their view in terms of knowledge, others in terms of justification or entitlement, still others in terms of warrant. Audi (1997, 1998, and 2006) embraces a non-reductionist view of testimonial knowledge, but not of testimonial justification. Stevenson (1993), Millgram (1997), and Graham (2006) defend restricted versions of non-reductionism.

[3]   Proponents of different versions of reductionism include Hume (1977), Fricker (1987, 1994, 1995, and 2006a, and 2006b), Adler (1994 and 2002), Lyons (1997), Lipton (1998), and Van Cleve (2006). Lehrer (2006) develops a qualified reductionist/non-reductionist view of testimonial justification.

which gives proper credence to testimony's epistemologically *dual* nature: in order to acquire testimonial justification, *both* the speaker and the hearer must make a *positive* epistemic contribution to the belief in question, the former through the reliability of her statement and the latter through her positive reasons. Thus, unlike non-reductionism, which places the epistemic burden almost entirely on the speaker, and reductionism, which places it on the hearer, dualism has the epistemic responsibility shared by both members of the testimonial exchange.

The second area in social epistemology to which I have contributed is the epistemology of disagreement. The question at the center of this literature is what the rational response should be to disagreement in situations where there are no relevant epistemic asymmetries between the members involved in the dispute, that is, when there is disagreement between *epistemic peers*. There are two main answers to this question. On the one hand, there is the view of the *conformists*,[4] who hold that, unless one has a reason that is independent of the disagreement itself to prefer one's own belief, one cannot continue to rationally believe that *p* when one is faced with an epistemic peer who explicitly believes that not-*p*. On the other hand, there is the view of the *nonconformists*,[5] who maintain that one can continue to rationally believe that *p* despite the fact that one's epistemic peer explicitly believes that not-*p*, even when one does not have a reason independent of the disagreement itself to prefer one's own belief. I have argued against both of these views and developed and defended an alternative view.[6]

The problem with the conformist view is that it seems to deliver the wrong result in some ordinary cases of disagreement. For instance, suppose that you and I are eating lunch together at a restaurant with a pitcher of water in the middle of the table, inches from each of us and in plain sight. Suppose further, however, that when I ask you to pass the pitcher to me so that I can pour a glass of water, you deny its existence. If, prior to this disagreement, neither you nor I had any reason to think that the other is evidentially or cognitively deficient in any way, and we both sincerely avowed our respective conflicting beliefs, how should I rationally respond to your claim here? Despite the fact that, up to now, I have had good reason to regard you as an epistemic peer, it seems clearly rational for me to continue to believe just as strongly that the pitcher is on the table. For given the extraordinarily high degree of justified

---

[4] Different versions of conformism can be found in Feldman (2006 and 2007), Christensen (2007 and 2011), and Elga (2007 and 2010).

[5] Various versions of nonconformism can be found in van Inwagen (1996 and 2010), Rosen (2001), Kelly (2005), Moffett (2007), Wedgewood (2007), and Bergmann (2009).

[6] See my (2010*a*, 2010*b*, and forthcoming).

confidence with which I hold my belief about the pitcher of water, your disagreement seems best taken as evidence that something has gone awry with you, either evidentially or cognitively.

The problem with the nonconformist view is that it seems to deliver the wrong result in other ordinary cases of disagreement. For instance, suppose that you and I are dining with three other friends and we all agree to leave a 20% tip and to evenly split the cost of the bill. You and I rightly regard one another as peers where calculations are concerned—we frequently dine together and consistently arrive at the same figure when dividing up the amount owed. After the bill arrives and we each have a clear look at it, I assert with confidence that I have carefully calculated in my head that we each owe $43 while you assert with the same degree of confidence that you have carefully calculated in your head that we each owe $45.[7] In such a case, it seems quite clear that rationality requires substantial belief revision on both of our parts until we are able to recheck our calculations. For barring any unusual circumstances, both you and I should recognize the likelihood that we could be wrong and that there is no reason to prefer our own beliefs to that of the other.

In place of both conformism and nonconformism, I have offered an alternate account of disagreement's epistemic significance that delivers the correct verdict in both of these sorts of cases. According to my *justificationist view*, the amount of doxastic revision required in peer disagreement tracks the degree to which the target belief is confidently held and highly justified and depends on whether the presence of what I call *personal information* is sufficient for breaking the epistemic symmetry between the parties to the dispute. Personal information is information that one has about the reliable functioning of one's own cognitive faculties. I may, for instance, know about myself that I have not recently had visual hallucinations, or that I am not currently experiencing side effects from prescribed medication, or that I am not severely sleep deprived or depressed, and so on, whereas I may not know that all of this is true of you. Thus, on my view, the cases where conformism clearly provides the correct result are ones where there is a relatively low degree of justified confidence such that the positive support provided by personal information is insufficient for breaking the epistemic symmetry between oneself and one's epistemic peer. In contrast, the cases where nonconformism clearly provides the correct result are ones where there is a symmetry breaker between one's epistemic peer and oneself that is provided by the presence of personal information combining with a highly justified confident belief. A central virtue of my justificationist

---

[7]   This sort of case can be found in Christensen (2007).

view, then, is that it offers a fully generalizable account of peer disagreement with principled and unifying explanations of intuitions that would otherwise appear to be in conflict.

The third area in social epistemology to which I have contributed is collective epistemology. There are two main views in this literature regarding the relationship between groups and the individual members who comprise them: while *deflationists*[8] about collective entities argue that groups and their states can simply be fleshed out in terms of individual members and their states, *inflationists*[9] maintain that groups and their states must be understood as over and above, or otherwise distinct from, individual members and their states. The only available deflationist view in the current literature is *summativism*, which holds that a group's state can be understood in the minimal sense that all or some members of the group are, or would be, in that state. So, for instance, on a deflationist, summative account of group belief or knowledge, a group's believing or knowing a proposition amounts to all or some members of the group believing or knowing that proposition. The classic version of inflationism in the literature is *non-summativism*, according to which a group's state cannot be understood in the sense that all or some members of the group are, or would be, in that state. Instead, the group itself is the bearer of the state. Such views in general are supported by *divergence arguments*, which purport to establish that phenomena at the group level can diverge from what is happening at the individual level among the group's members. For instance, the divergence arguments with respect to group belief and group knowledge hold that a group can be properly said to believe or know a proposition even if not a single one of its members believes or knows it. This might happen, for example, when a department agrees to put forward a candidate as the best applicant for admission to their Ph.D. program, despite the fact that not a single one of its members actually believes this is correct; instead, they all think that this is the candidate who is most likely to be approved by the administration. In such a case, the inflationist, non-summative accounts of group belief and knowledge take this to be a good reason to accept that the department itself, rather than any particular individual(s), believes or knows this proposition.

Interest in collective epistemology has grown considerably in recent years, but nearly all of the work done in this area has been shaped by the view that divergence arguments have decisively established inflationism about collective phenomena. In my forthcoming book on groups, I

---

8   See Quinton (1975/1976) for the classic presentation of deflationism.

9   See Gilbert (1989), Tuomela (1992), Schmitt (1994), Pettit (2003), Tollefsen (2007 and 2009), and Bird (2010) for different versions of inflationism.

argue that this conclusion is false and rests on the mistaken assumption that the failure of summativism thereby undermines deflationism. What I show, however, is that although divergence arguments work against summative accounts, they do not establish inflationism with respect to group phenomena. Thus, it has hitherto been unnoticed that there is room for an altogether different sort of view in collective epistemology—one that is *both deflationist and non-summative*. On my view, it is not just individuals and their states that determine group phenomena, but also the *relations that exist between them* and the *social environment in which such individuals are located*. Thus, I show that the states of collective entities cannot be understood in the minimal sense that all or some members of the group are, or would be, in that state, but this does not mean that the states are over and above that of individuals in any sort of inflationary sense.

3. What is the proper role of social epistemology in relation to other disciplines?

Social epistemology is connected to, and plays a crucial role in, many disciplines. To name just a few, questions of how to interpret history often depend heavily on our understanding of the epistemic states of collective entities. When it is said that Britain intentionally sank the *Belgrano* during the Falklands War, for example, the truth of this claim turns on how we understand the collective entity, Britain, and its capacity for intentional states. Many legal debates turn on the question of whether groups, such as corporations, can possess the knowledge needed to satisfy *mens rea*. For instance, is it possible for a nursing home to knowingly kill a patient through improper care, or is this simply a shorthand way of saying that particular employees knew that the care being provided was grossly inadequate? And how to assess the highly collaborative nature of much scientific inquiry is clearly affected by our understanding of the epistemic status of testimony. For example, if seventy-five authors are involved in the publication of a new kind of treatment for Alzheimer's, many of whom have never met one another and simply conveyed the results of their research to the group via e-mail, are their testimonial beliefs justified even if they lack the full range of positive reasons for them?

One concrete example of the close connection between social epistemology and other disciplines—in particular, that found between collective epistemology, the law, and business ethics—can be seen by considering the following: on March 6, 1984, the United States Department of Defense charged that between 1978 and 1981 the company National Semiconductor had sold them twenty-six million computer chips that had not been properly tested and then had falsified their records to conceal the fraud.[10] These potentially defective chips had been used in airplane guidance systems, nuclear weapons systems, guided missiles, rocket launchers, and other sensitive military equipment. Highlighting the gravity of the situation, a government official noted that if one of these computer chips malfunctioned, "You could have a missile that would end up in Cleveland instead of the intended target."

Officials at National Semiconductor admitted to both the omission of required tests and the falsification of relevant documentation and agreed to pay $1.75 million in penalties for defrauding the government. However, the company refused to provide the names of any of the individuals who had participated in the decision to omit the tests and falsify the documents, or any who had been involved in carrying out these tasks. The legal counsel for the Department of Defense objected, arguing that "a corporation acts only through its employees and officers" and thus the government would have no assurance that National Semiconductor would not engage in the fraud again. In response, the CEO of National Semiconductor said, "We totally disagree with the Defense Department's proposal. We have repeatedly stated that we accept responsibility as a company and we steadfastly continue to stand by that statement." A spokesperson for National Semiconductor later reiterated this position: "We will see [that our individual people] are not harmed. We feel it's a company responsibility, [and this is] a matter of ethics." National Semiconductor prevailed: no individual employee was ever held criminally or civilly liable for the crime. Only the company *qua* company was penalized.

The tension that we see in this case between the responsibility of the group and that of the individual members lies at the heart of the debate between deflationists and inflationists mentioned earlier. Moreover, making sense of whether the deflationist or the inflationist provides the correct view of this sort of case depends on first resolving more foundational issues in collective epistemology, such as understanding the nature of *group belief*, *group knowledge*, and *group testimony*. If National Semiconductor is to be treated as an entity over and above its members in bearing responsibility for defrauding the government, for instance, then it is essential to determine whether the company believed or knew that required tests were being omitted and relevant documentation falsified and whether it testified to its employees that such tasks should be carried out. Thus, the accounts offered in collective epistemology of these crucial notions will shed light on whether it is groups, their individual members, or both who ought to be held legally and/or morally responsible for actions.

---

[10] This case, including all of the quotations, are from Velasquez (2003).

4. What have been the most significant advances in social epistemology?

There have been many significant advances in social epistemology, a number with implications that reach far beyond philosophy, from Goldman's work on expertise and paternalism to developments in the judgment aggregation literature on the discursive dilemma. But one recent advance is the conversation started by the publication of Miranda Fricker's book, *Epistemic Injustice: Power and the Ethics of Knowing*. According to Fricker, testimonial injustice is distinctively epistemic in nature and occurs when someone is wronged in her capacity as a knower via prejudice. While it has always been clear that prejudice can result in various kinds of ethical injustices, that it can also produce epistemic harm is indeed an important point to emphasize. For it reminds us all to tread carefully when assessing the testimony of those likely to be victims of such injustice, especially when it comes into conflict with the reports of others.

Another important development in social epistemology is the attention that is being devoted to the relevance of peer disagreement to knowledge. It is uncontroversial that counterevidence can defeat the justification we have for beliefs, but if peer disagreement is counterevidence of this sort, then our conflicts with others might be the most powerful and prevalent defeaters that there are. Yet few of us in practice treat the conflicting views of our peers as reason to give up our beliefs. If this is indeed irrational, as some have argued, then this area of social epistemology is calling our attention to arguably one of the greatest deficiencies of our epistemic lives. Moreover, disagreement also sheds light on the epistemic power, and perhaps limitations, of the testimony of others. Should we, for instance, be as inclined to withhold belief when a peer disagrees with us about whether eating nonhuman animals is morally wrong as we are when she disagrees with us that the animal at a zoo is an echidna rather than a hedgehog? If not—if disagreement regarding moral and perhaps other normative matters does not carry as much epistemic weight as it does in other areas—then perhaps the testimony of others has weaknesses that other epistemic sources do not.

5. What are the most important open problems in social epistemology and what are the prospects for progress?

There are many important open problems in social epistemology, but one area that I think is of particular interest and has the potential to bear much fruit is the examination of concrete issues, both in philosophy and in other disciplines, through the lens of developments in social epistemology—what we might call *applied social epistemology*. I already mentioned one such instance above, where questions in the law and business ethics about whether National Semiconductor, its individual employees, or both ought to be held responsible for the fraudulent actions can be illuminated by work in collective epistemology. But another example that has received very little attention is the relationship between disciplines that depend heavily on the reports of others—history, the law, science, and so on—and competing views in the epistemology of testimony and disagreement.

I began thinking about some of these connections when I collaborated with a lawyer and a historian to teach an interdisciplinary course on testimony and justice, looking at the epistemological questions that arise when testimony is being offered in the aim of justice, such as reports offered at International Criminal Tribunals regarding mass rapes and from the perpetrators and survivors of the Holocaust. For instance, when what we learn about certain historical events is indebted to historians who are themselves entirely dependent on the testimony of those involved, how justified are we in forming the corresponding beliefs? Christopher Browning, a historian writing about a police battalion of Germans who murdered tens of thousands of Jews during WWII, raises this question directly in the following:

In writing about Reserve Police Battalion 101...I have depended heavily upon the judicial interrogations of some 125 men conducted in the 1960s. To read about the same events experienced by a single unit as filtered through the memories of 125 different men more than twenty years after the fact is disconcerting to a historian looking for certainties. Each of these men played a different role. He saw and did different things. Each subsequently repressed or forgot certain aspects of the battalion's experiences, or reshaped his memory of them in a different way. Thus the interrogations inevitably present a confusing array of perspectives and memories. Paradoxically, I would have had the illusion of being more certain about what happened to the battalion with one detailed recollection instead of 125...

As with the use of multiple sources, the many accounts and perspectives had to be sifted and weighed. The reliability of each witness had to be assessed. Much of the testimony had to be partially or totally dismissed in favor of conflicting testimony that was accepted. Many of these judgments were both straightforward and obvious, but others were quite difficult. And as self-conscious as I have tried to be, at times I undoubtedly made purely instinctive judgments without even being aware of it. Other historians looking at the same materials would retell these events in somewhat different ways. (Browning 1992, pp. xviii-xix)

As these passages make clear, our understanding of these murders depends on both the reliability of the testimony offered by the 125 men in Reserve Police Battalion 101 and on Browning's own interpretation of their reports. Disagreement arises at both levels as well: the members of the battalion provided conflicting testimony of the same events, and other historians disagree with Browning's presentation of them. How does this affect our ability to acquire knowledge here? How do we apportion epistemic responsibility to the original testifiers, the historian, and the recipients of the testimony? Clearly, whether non-reductionism, reductionism, or dualism is correct in the epistemology of testimony, and whether conformism, non-conformism, or justificationism is right in the epistemology of disagreement, bears directly on these questions.

To my mind, the next step in social epistemology is to flesh these connections out, to show how developments in social epistemology bear on our understanding of concrete issues in the law, business ethics, history, and beyond. Given that the importance of interdisciplinary work is increasingly appreciated in philosophy, I think the prospects for progress here are excellent.[11]

References

Adler, Jonathan E.

> 1994. "Testimony, Trust, Knowing." *The Journal of Philosophy* 91: 264-75.

> 2002. *Belief's Own Ethics*. Cambridge, MA: The MIT Press.

Audi, Robert.

> 1997. "The Place of Testimony in the Fabric of Knowledge and Justification." *American Philosophical Quarterly* 34: 405-22.

> 1998. *Epistemology: A Contemporary Introduction to the Theory of Knowledge*. London: Routledge.

> 2006. "Testimony, Credulity, and Veracity," in Jennifer Lackey and Ernest Sosa (eds.), *The Epistemology of Testimony*. Oxford: Oxford University Press: 25-49.

Austin, J.L. 1979. "Other Minds," in his *Philosophical Papers*, 3rd edn. Oxford: Oxford University Press.

Bergmann, Michael. 2009. "Rational Disagreement after Full Disclosure." *Episteme* 6: 336-53.

Bird, Alexander. 2010. "Social Knowing: The Social Sense of 'Scientific Knowledge'." *Philosophical Perspectives* 24: 23-56.

---

[11] I am indebted, as always, to invaluable conversations with Baron Reed on the topics discussed in these answers.

Browning, Christopher. 1992. *Ordinary Men: Reserve Police Battalion 101 and the Final Solution in Poland*. New York: HarperCollins Publishers.

Burge, Tyler.
    1993. "Content Preservation." *The Philosophical Review* 102: 457-488.

    1997. "Interlocution, Perception, and Memory." *Philosophical Studies* 86: 21-47.

Christensen, David.
    2007. "Epistemology of Disagreement: the Good News." *The Philosophical Review* 116: 187-217.

    2011. "Disagreement, Question-Begging and Epistemic Self-Criticism." *Philosophers' Imprint* 11.

Coady, C.A.J.
    1992. *Testimony: A Philosophical Study*. Oxford: Clarendon Press.

    1994. "Testimony, Observation and 'Autonomous Knowledge'," in Bimal Krishna Matilal and Arindam Chakrabarti (eds.), *Knowing from Words*. Dordrecht: Kluwer Academic Publishers: 225-50.

Dummett, Michael. 1994. "Testimony and Memory," in Bimal Krishna Matilal and Arindam

Chakrabarti (eds.), *Knowing from Words*. Dordrecht: Kluwer Academic Publishers: 251-72.

Elga, Adam
    2007. "Reflection and Disagreement." *Noûs* 41: 478-502.

    2010. "How to Disagree About How to Disagree" in Richard Feldman and Ted Warfield (eds.), *Disagreement*. Oxford: Oxford University Press.

Evans, Gareth. 1982. *The Varieties of Reference*. Oxford: Clarendon Press.

Faulkner, Paul. 2006. "On Dreaming and Being Lied To." *Episteme* 3: 149-59.

Feldman, Richard.
    2006. "Epistemological Puzzles about Disagreement" in Stephen Hetherington (ed.), *Epistemology Futures*. Oxford: Oxford University Press, pp. 216-36.

    2007. "Reasonable Religious Disagreements" in Louise Antony (ed.), *Philosophers without Gods: Meditations on Atheism and the Secular Life*. Oxford: Oxford University Press.

Foley, Richard. 1994. "Egoism in Epistemology," in Frederick F. Schmitt (ed.), *Socializing Epistemology: The Social Dimensions of Knowledge*. Lanham, MD: Rowman and Littlefield: 53-73.

Fricker, Elizabeth.
>   1987. "The Epistemology of Testimony." *Proceedings of the Aristotelian Society,* supp. vol. 61: 57-83.

>   1994. "Against Gullibility," in Bimal Krishna Matilal and Arindam Chakrabarti (eds.), *Knowing from Words*. Dordrecht: Kluwer Academic Publishers: 125-61.

>   1995. "Telling and Trusting: Reductionism and Anti-Reductionism in the Epistemology of Testimony." *Mind* 104: 393-411.

>   2006*a*. "Testimony and Epistemic Autonomy," in Jennifer Lackey and Ernest Sosa (eds.), *The Epistemology of Testimony*. Oxford: Oxford University Press: 225-50.

>   2006*b*. "Knowledge from Trust in Testimony is Second-Hand Knowledge." *Philosophy and Phenomenological Research* 73: 592-618.

Fricker, Miranda. 2007. *Epistemic Injustice: Power and the Ethics of Knowing*. Oxford: Oxford University Press.

Gilbert, Margaret.
>   1989. *On Social Facts*. London and New York: Routledge.

>   1994. "Remarks on Collective Belief," in Frederick F. Schmitt (ed.), *Socializing Epistemology: The Social Dimensions of Knowledge*. Lanham, MD: Rowman & Littlefield: 235-55.

Goldberg, Sanford C. 2010. *Relying on Others: An Essay in Epistemology*. Oxford: Oxford University Press.

Goldman, Alvin I. 1999. *Knowledge in a Social World*. Oxford: Clarendon Press.

Graham, Peter J. 2006. "Liberal Fundamentalism and Its Rivals," in Jennifer Lackey and Ernest Sosa (eds.), *The Epistemology of Testimony*. Oxford: Oxford University Press: 93-115.

Hardwig, John.
>   1985. "Epistemic Dependence." *The Journal of Philosophy* 82: 335-49.

>   1991. "The Role of Trust in Knowledge." *The Journal of Philosophy* 88: 693-708.

Hume, David. 1977. *An Enquiry Concerning Human Understanding*, Eric Steinberg (ed.). Indianapolis: Hackett.

Kelly, Thomas. 2005. "The Epistemic Significance of Disagreement" in John Hawthorne and Tamar Szabo Gendler (eds.), *Oxford Studies in Epistemology, volume* 1. Oxford: Oxford University Press, pp. 167-196.

Lackey, Jennifer.

2008 *Learning from Words*. Oxford: Oxford University Press.

2010*a*. "A Justificationist View of Disagreement's Epistemic Significance," in Adrian Haddock, Alan Millar, and Duncan Pritchard (eds.), *Social Epistemology*. Oxford: Oxford University Press.

2010*b*. "What Should We Do When We Disagree," in Tamar Szabó Gendler and John Hawthorne (eds.), *Oxford Studies in Epistemology*. Oxford: Oxford University Press.

(Forthcoming) "Disagreement and Belief Dependence: Why Numbers Matter," in David Christensen and Jennifer Lackey (eds.), *The Epistemology of Disagreement: New Essays* (Oxford: Oxford University Press).

Lehrer, Keith. 2006. "Testimony and Trustworthiness," in Jennifer Lackey and Ernest Sosa (eds.), *The Epistemology of Testimony*. Oxford: Oxford University Press: 145-59.

Lipton, Peter. 1998. "The Epistemology of Testimony." *Studies in History and Philosophy of Science* 29: 1-31.

Lyons, Jack. 1997. "Testimony, Induction and Folk Psychology." *Australasian Journal of Philosophy* 75: 163-78.

McDowell, John. 1994. "Knowledge by Hearsay," in Bimal Krishna Matilal and Arindam Chakrabarti (eds.), *Knowing from Words*. Dordrecht: Kluwer Academic Publishers: 195-224.

Millgram, Elijah. 1997. *Practical Induction*. Cambridge, MA: Harvard University Press.

Moffett, Marc. 2007. "Reasonable Disagreement and Rational Group Inquiry." *Episteme* 4: 352-67.

Owens, David.

2000. *Reason without Freedom: The Problem of Epistemic Normativity*. London: Routledge.

2006. "Testimony and Assertion." *Philosophical Studies* 130: 105-29.

Pettit, Philip. (2003) "Groups with Minds of Their Own," in Frederick Schmitt (ed.), *Socializing Metaphysics*. New York: Rowman and Littlefield: 167-93.

Plantinga, Alvin. 1993. *Warrant and Proper Function*. Oxford: Oxford University Press.

Quinton, Anthony. (1975/1976) "Social Objects." *Proceedings of the Aristotelian Society* 75: 1–27.

Reid, Thomas. 1983. *Essay on the Intellectual Powers of Man*, in Ronald E. Beanblossom and Keith Lehrer (eds.), *Thomas Reid's Inquiry and Essays*. Indianapolis: Hackett.

Reynolds, Steven L. 2002. "Testimony, Knowledge, and Epistemic Goals." *Philosophical Studies* 110: 139-61.

Rosen, Gideon. 2001. "Nominalism, Naturalism, Epistemic Relativism." *Philosophical Perspectives* 15: 69-91.

Ross, Angus. 1986. "Why Do We Believe What We Are Told?" *Ratio* 28: 69-88.

Rysiew, Patrick. 2002. "Testimony, Simulation, and the Limits of Inductivism." *Australasian Journal of Philosophy* 78: 269-74.

Schmitt, Frederick F.
    (1994) "The Justification of Group Beliefs," in Frederick F. Schmitt (ed.), *Socializing Epistemology: The Social Dimensions of Knowledge*. Lanham, MD: Rowman & Littlefield: 257-87.

    1999. "Social Epistemology," in John Greco and Ernest Sosa (eds.), *The Blackwell Guide to Epistemology*. Oxford: Blackwell Publishers: 354-82.

    2006. "Testimonial Justification and Transindividual Reasons," in Jennifer Lackey and Ernest Sosa (eds.), *The Epistemology of Testimony*. Oxford: Oxford University Press: 193-224.

Sosa, Ernest. 2006. "Knowledge: Instrumental and Testimonial," in Jennifer Lackey and Ernest Sosa (eds.), *The Epistemology of Testimony*. Oxford: Oxford University Press: 116-23.

Stevenson, Leslie. 1993. "Why Believe What People Say?" *Synthese* 94: 429-51.

Strawson, P.F. 1994. "Knowing From Words," in Bimal Krishna Matilal and Arindam Chakrabarti (eds.), *Knowing from Words*. Dordrecht: Kluwer Academic Publishers: 23-27.

Tollefsen, Deborah.
    2007. "Group Testimony." *Social Epistemology* 21: 299-311.

    2009. "*Wikipedia* and the Epistemology of Testimony." *Episteme* 6: 8-24.

Tuomela, Raimo. 1992. "Group Beliefs." *Synthese* 91: 285-318.

van Inwagen, Peter.
    1996. "It is Wrong, Everywhere, Always, and for Anyone, to

Believe Anything on Insufficient Evidence," in Jeff Jordan and Daniel Howard-Snyder (eds.), *Faith, Freedom, and Rationality: Philosophy of Religion Today*. London: Rowman and Littlefield, pp.137-153.

2010. "We're Right, They're Wrong," in Richard Feldman and Ted Warfield (eds.), *Disagreement*. Oxford: Oxford University Press.

Van Cleve, James. 2006. "Reid on the Credit of Human Testimony," in Jennifer Lackey and Ernest Sosa (eds.), *The Epistemology of Testimony*. Oxford: Oxford University Press: 50-74.

Velasquez, Manuel. 2003. "Debunking Corporate Responsibility." *Business Ethics Quarterly* 13: 531-62.

Webb, Mark Owen. 1993. "Why I Know About As Much As You: A Reply to Hardwig." *The Journal of Philosophy* 110: 260-70.

Wedgwood, Ralph. 2007. *The Nature of Normativity*. Oxford: Oxford University Press.

Weiner, Matthew. 2003. "Accepting Testimony." *The Philosophical Quarterly* 53: 256-64.

Welbourne, Michael.
2 1979. "The Transmission of Knowledge." *The Philosophical Quarterly* 29: 1-9.

1981. "The Community of Knowledge." *The Philosophical Quarterly* 31: 302-14.

1986. *The Community of Knowledge*. Aberdeen: Aberdeen University Press.

1994. "Testimony, Knowledge and Belief," in Bimal Krishna Matilal and Arindam Chakrabarti (eds.), *Knowing from Words*. Dordrecht: Kluwer Academic Publishers: 297-313.

Williamson, Timothy.
1996. "Knowing and Asserting." *The Philosophical Review* 105: 489-523.

2000. *Knowledge and its Limits*. Oxford: Oxford University Press.

13

Helen E. Longino

Professor of Philosophy
Stanford University

---

1. Why were you initially drawn to social epistemology?

In the late 1970s I was trying to reconcile the implications of my analysis of evidential relations with a conviction that the sciences were characterized by some kind of methodological guarantee of objectivity. The problem was generated by an analysis of then standard accounts of hypothesis confirmation. It turned out that these accounts could only apply to situations in which hypothesis and data statements shared all descriptive terms. Confirmation was basically represented as a relation between a generalization and its instances. But generalizations of observation statements form only a small part of the evidential situations in the sciences. The bulk of evidential claims in the sciences concern hypotheses that would explain observed phenomena by appeal to processes quite different in character from those requiring explanation. The explanatory processes are undergone by entities too small or too distant in space or time or generally other than the entities whose behavior is the subject of inquiry. For example, genes (or heritable factors, as they were initially called) are different than the phenotypes of peas – yellowish vs. greenish in color, wrinkled vs. smooth — that Mendel studied. Analysis of the formal situation indicated that the evidential relevance of data to particular hypotheses was a function of background assumptions connecting the data to those hypotheses (and not to others).

Although I did not know it under this description at the time, I had talked myself into the problem of underdetermination, as French physicist and philosopher Pierre Duhem had expressed it back at the turn of the 20th century. But there was more to the problem. If evidential relevance was not a matter of formal relations holding between theories or hypotheses and data, there was no formal way to prevent values or preferences from being motivated by or expressed in those assumptions. If this were so, there was then no formal way to guarantee the value-freedom of the sciences. I can remember being struck, sitting at my desk one afternoon, by the thought that we were only victims of our (unknown) values and prejudices if we thought in a vacuum, unhindered by discursive relations with others. Objectivity could be saved if we understood it as a function not of some kind of pure relation of cognizers with our subject matter, but as a function of intersubjective criticism.

I felt pulled back from the brink, but details were required in order to see how this insight could be incorporated into an account of scientific knowledge. There were two aspects to this. One was to think about the nature and conditions of criticism. I knew well that criticism alone was not sufficient, as one could be critical until blue in the face and it make no difference to the belief patterns of the community. Another was to think about how this might be reflected in the practices (or aspirations) of scientists. The view I call critical contextual empiricism is my still developing effort to work out these questions.

2. What are your main contributions to the field of social epistemology?

As I just outlined, my work in social epistemology started out in problems connected to scientific knowledge, that is, in problems about knowledge (truth, objectivity) gained through inquiry in a field that was already thoroughly social. Scientific knowledge was produced by scientific communities, not by individuals, and I saw this as the solution to problems generated by underdetermination considerations, rather than as a challenge to some existing account of knowledge. This is a very different problem space than the space occupied by epistemologists concerned with the status of testimony or with the proper response to disagreement. (More about this below.) Nevertheless, I had to contend with approaches to scientific knowledge that took the individual cognizer as the primary knower and that offered analyses of epistemological concepts such as evidence and confirmation that presupposed the epistemological self-sufficiency of individuals. My solution to the problem of objectivity posed by underdetermination required that we not take the individual as the primary unit in the epistemology of science.

In *Science as Social Knowledge* I laid out the case for the role of background assumptions and for the role of intersubjective criticism in controlling the influence of subjective preferences. Because descriptions of data that served as evidence and the hypotheses for which the data were taken as evidence were about different kinds of object and articulated in different terms, there could be no formal account of the relation between evidence and hypothesis. On the other hand, I had long been convinced by my graduate advisor (Peter Achinstein) that the Kuhnian/Feyerabendian account of theory determination of observation was as problematic as the empiricist account of observation determination of theory. There had to be another way, and for me that was the contextualist line: data constitute evidence for particular hypotheses in the context of assumptions that establish the relevance of the data to the hypotheses.

It is the "critical" in critical contextual empiricism that constitutes the turn to the social. I have offered three kinds of argument for the social character of knowledge: one is that this is the solution to the problem of objectivity, a second that this better reflects the objectivity-oriented practices of the sciences themselves, a third that the cognitive practices of the sciences themselves (and of empirical knowledge more generally) are social practices. With respect to the first point, I argued that without some strategy for detecting the values or value-laden considerations that could ride in on the background assumptions needed to support evidential reasoning, scientific conclusions were vulnerable to being biased or influenced by shared or below threshold values. This was illustrated by examples of scientific reasoning that passed muster among scientific peers, but either was clearly influenced by value-laden considerations or resulted in the acceptance of hypotheses that were socially freighted. Gender bias in ethology, evolution, and human development was the easiest to demonstrate, although I also used examples from the history of science and from then current work on the biological effects of radiation exposure to demonstrate both how contextual values could enter into the scientific process and how critical interaction could make them visible and subject to evaluation. Only if such critical interaction were incorporated into our accounts of scientific method, that is, only if the process by which contextual values were identified and evaluated were treated as an explicit feature of scientific method, could it be claimed that these methods included means of keeping subjective preferences at bay.

This raises the question: why should critical interaction count as knowledge providing or justification providing? Radical critics of political pluralism had pointed out that tolerance of criticism carried no guarantee of its having any effect. Clearly what was required was mutual engagement. This is why the incorporation of criticism into an empiricist epistemology turns it into a social epistemology. Once this deep social turn was taken, norms applying to the social, interactive, dimension of knowledge-seeking inquiry would be needed. Such norms would not displace empiricist norms, e.g. those that treat observational data as the least defeasible grounds of hypothesis acceptance, and that recommend consistency or avoidance of contradiction. They would be additions to the norms. I articulated four norms of social cognitive practice, norms that (if one accepts the story so far) are binding on communities. I argued that satisfaction of these these (or something like them) was necessary in order that critical interaction be effective and community practices deserve classification as objective. The norms include 1) the community in which critical interaction takes place must provide recognized venues for critical interaction, 2) it must exhibit uptake of criticism in the sense that the beliefs of the community change in ways that are logically sensitive to the critical discourse taking place within it, 3) there must be public standards to which criticism and its responses are accountable, and 4) the community must be characterized by equality of intellectual authority (meaning that no perspective can be excluded prior to participation in the critical arena, although perspectives may lose status through violation of the standards). There are a number of consequences that follow from this analysis. One is that scientific communities must be diverse in order to generate criticism that can access deeply held and shared assumptions. They must also be open to criticism from outside the community. Another is that objectivity is first of all a property of a community of inquirers and only derivatively of individual members of the community and secondly turns out to be a matter of degree, as the conditions can be differentially satisfied. A third is that knowledge may be no less knowledge for being plural in character.

The second kind of argument focused attention on the sciences themselves. Scientists and apologists for the sciences claim that one distinguishing feature of the sciences is their openness to criticism. Why should this be an important feature if it is not understood as contributing to attaining the professed goal of inquiry: knowledge (of the natural and social worlds)? And, indeed, when we examine the sciences, we see that they are themselves intensely social. This feature has been given an anti-cognitive interpretation in some sociological circles. These anti-cognitive interpretations include an emphasis on the practical, technological, goals the sciences help societies achieve, as well as suggestions that all scientific disputes are settled by negotiation or exercises of power. Of this, more below. But minimally, the sciences are characterized by educational practices for transmitting and exchanging traditions of practice, and, in the modern period, advanced by the communication of ideas, experiments, and results.

In the 17th century, letters passed by the agency of figures like Mersenne and Oldenbaugh were crucial to the development of the new sciences, as were communications to newly formed academies like the Royal Society. These letters and communications were not just taken as additions to a body of information, but as proposals to be discussed, debated, criticized, examined for their coherence and plausibility. Subsequent philosophers, mesmerized by Descartes' Meditations, have focused on the dilemma of the solitary figure by the fire, discarding all his beliefs until he can find at least one thing he cannot doubt. But Descartes himself was part of a network of intellectuals, in the very difficult circumstances of 17th century politics, together forging the beginnings of modern science. What we have taken as his philosophy and what seems to be his practice of knowledge are at odds with each other.

These days, the peer review practices of journals and the conventions of conference participation, signal the importance of critical scrutiny of reports of experiments and reflection on their significance prior to their acceptance as results that can be relied on by others.. While the actual implementation of peer review can be and has been criticized (for favoring reputation over substance, for example), the ideals of peer review testify to the importance given to criticism from different perspectives. The sciences themselves are organized socially and certain epistemologically relevant practices, that is, practices that are taken to guarantee the doxastic trustworthiness of the sciences, are social practices. In addition to practices of peer review, norms of repeatability of studies and experiments, of subjection to examination through publication in professional journals, are key features of this trustworthiness. That these norms are violated, for example, in agreements with private funders of research, through patterns of publication and funding that favor highly ranked institutions, through the lesser attention paid to negative results, through announcing results in press conferences rather than through standard professional channels is not evidence that the norms are not recognized. Instead, the fact that instances of such practices are condemned as violations of a scientific ethos or their spread seen as a problem for the professions is evidence that the norms are accepted as norms. Both the history of modern science and its current practices, then, offer materials for an argument that the reasons the sciences can be represented as objective include features of their social practices, and not just the satisfaction of norms of reasoning and observation applicable to individuals. And, if this is so, then our epistemology must encompass those social practices taken to contribute to the epistemic goals of scientific inquiry.

The third kind of argument was developed in The Fate of Knowledge. There I argued that cognitive practices taken to be constitutive of (empirical) knowledge, observation and justificatory reasoning, are social practices. Observation employs concepts and categories whose extensions and boundaries must be socially agreed upon. Observations must be shareable, public, in order to count as observations. Thus, the kind of sensory information that counts as evidence is not private, internal to the sensing individual, or incorrigible, but is commonable, referenced to a public object of perception, and described and classified in terms whose meanings are socially instituted and maintained. Justificatory reasoning, the kind of reasoning involved in hypothesis confirmation, I argued, gets its point in a context of challenge and response. Furthermore, the dependence of evidential relevance on background assumptions means that reasoning that may seem to be performed by individuals is conducted in a context of shared assumptions. In Fate, I also argued that certain understandings of the concept of truth were too restricted to encompass the kinds of semantic success expected of the sciences and inappropriate to certain kinds of scientific content. I proposed the concept of 'conformation' instead, as a cover term for notions such as resemblance, approximation, isomorphism, homomorphism — and truth. Once semantic and, dare I say it, epistemic success, is broadened in these ways, it requires specification of respects and degrees—the respects in which a representation must resemble, approximate, etc., that which it is purported to represent and the degree to which it must resemble, approximate, etc. These specifications are socially determined. Once determined (along with acceptable error bars, etc.), whether they are satisfied is independent of the social processes that go into the determination. But social interaction is a key feature of determining what will qualify as success.

These three kinds of argument mean that the normative concerns of epistemology, the questions about distinguishing knowledge from belief or opinion, must be directed to community practices, and not just to the practices of individuals. To the extent that we take the sciences to be exemplars of empirical knowledge, these arguments extend the social to empirical knowledge, generally. Some adjustments must be made for the difference between the institutionalized sociality that characterizes the sciences, and the informal sociality that characterizes our more everyday cognitive endeavors, but the arguments of Fate are applicable outside of the scientific context. Furthermore, making knowledge constitutively social opens a social alternative to the social constructivist view that treats the sciences as (merely) a play of interests and power. Certainly, interests and power are at work in scientific communities, but opening our conception of scientific methodology to include the social dimensions of science shows that the sciences also have means of mitigating their influence. The social analysis does not eliminate the roles of empirical data and of logic, but integrates them into a fuller picture of scientific method. The social is not an enemy of objectivity, but a means of attaining it. Social epistemology, which shows how the traditional normative concerns of philosophers are achieved through social interaction, can cooperate with the sociological investigation of cognitive practices rather than being irrelevant or antagonistic.

3. What is the proper role of social epistemology in relation to other disciplines?

As the above makes clear, I think social epistemology is crucial for a proper understanding of scientific knowledge and that it provides the basic ingredients for a proper understanding of empirical knowledge more generally. Because we take the sciences to be paragons of objectivity, the results of social epistemology are important for any other cognitive activity of which we expect objectivity. And, once objectivity is understood as a feature of process rather than of content fitting its object, then social epistemology becomes a field of very wide scope, including ethics and social and political philosophy. Indeed, if one takes the claims of sociality far enough, it becomes relevant to mathematical and logical knowledge, as well. I have suggested as much in the conclusion of *The Fate of Knowledge*, but have not as yet developed the idea. So social epistemology is relevant to the problems of other areas of philosophy. But there are questions social epistemology provokes that other areas of philosophy can help us think about. For example, what is the ontological status of groups? Should we think of knowers, cognitive agents, as primarily individuals (in community) or as communities. What hangs on this distinction? And, what counts as community? Do communities have fixed boundaries? Certainly their memberships overlap. What features of communities might be of relevance in thinking normatively about their cognitive practices? Do the requirements of internal diversity and openness to criticism from outside undermine or reinforce each other? Such questions are of great relevance to an epistemology that puts community deliberations at its center. Political philosophers concerned with democratic process have reflected on the efficacy of deliberation, on the conditions of effective deliberation, on potential limits on participation. Their analyses have implications for the soundness and applicability of the kinds of norms I have proposed. And beyond philosophy, as I indicated, social epistemology has implications for the empirical disciplines concerned with knowledge and belief, both psychology and sociology. Furthermore, it requires that cognitive science include attention to social interactions and not just to intra-individual processes.

4. What have been the most significant advances in social epistemology?

Perhaps the most significant advance has been the emergence of social epistemology itself as a focus of sustained philosophical inquiry. Hume raised questions about testimony in his *Enquiry into Human Understanding*, and 224 years later, C.A.J. Coady revived serious discussion of testimony with the publication of his *Testimony*. Coady's book has given rise to a lively set of discussions about the status of testimony and of disagreement in epistemology. For many philosophers, these discussions are what constitute social epistemology. But philosophers of science and a few epistemologists attending to the conditions of acquisition and spread of knowledge have shown that there are additional deep and interesting philosophical issues to be pursued in thinking about the social dimensions of knowledge. Philip Kitcher and Alvin Goldman initiated a lively literature about the distribution of cognitive labor and about the authority of expertise. These are issues that still take individuals to be the primary agents of cognition, and they were at least initially pursued in philosophical frameworks committed to thinking of cognitive practices as in principle activities of individual cognitive agents. This opens up an interesting tension between approaches in social epistemology that conceive the problem space as constructed by the fact that individual knowers live in social contexts that affect their cognitive practices and approaches that conceive the problem space as constructed by the insolubility of epistemological problems when conceived in terms of individual agents only.

5. What are the most important open problems in social epistemology and what are the prospects for progress?

I just mentioned the tension between individualist and community forms of social epistemology. One important problem is understanding the relation between these two strands. One might think that they are separate undertakings, different parts of an epistemological investigation into the multifaceted social dimensions of knowledge. But they overlap in important and disconcerting ways. Take disagreement. One of the assumptions that makes disagreement a philosophical problem is the assumption that individuals are (ideally) cognitively self-sufficient and must possess a significant degree of self-trust. That is, they must trust their own cognitive practices. Absent some confidence in one's own observation and reasoning practices it's not even reasonable to engage in the kind of critical interaction that my form of social epistemology envisions. And, in the sciences, disagreement is commonplace. But in the standard examples, disagreement over such mundane matters as the correct division of a restaurant bill or whether there are 9 or 13 persons in the room, the fact of disagreement is a source of deep puzzlement. How can my companion come up with such a different conclusion to a simple matter? And what ought to be my response to this situation? One problem with the way the standard examples are cast is that the disagreements are often between a correct claim and an incorrect claim. It might be more fruitful to set these examples up as conflicts between claims that are both different from that which a standard well-informed, arithmetically competent, reader would take to be correct. Setting this reservation aside, it seems clear that the puzzle arises in part because of an assumption that cognitive processes are all in the head, and, as in the head, mutually inaccessible to the parties to a disagreement. What difference to the representation of disagreement would it make if cognitive processes are understood as (at least partially) social? Or consider testimony. The sciences progress, to the extent they do, because they can take some things as settled. It is not necessary to reconstruct the whole of a discipline *de novo* in order to add to the store of knowledge. Of course, the social epistemologist points to the practices of criticism, survival of which are a precondition of being taken as settled. But reliance on the work of others is necessary to the growth of knowledge. From this point of view, the issue is not whether testimony is reliable, but under what conditions it can serve not as grounds for accepting the content of the testimony, but as part of a set of grounds for some other conclusion. It seems to me that one important family of open problems concerns how to reconcile these different treatments of social epistemological phenomena. Consideration of these problems should yield some interesting philosophy.

14

Philip Pettit

L.S.Rockefeller University Professor of Politics and Human
Values, Princeton University AND Distinguished Professor of
Philosophy, Australian National University

Princeton University and Australian National University

---

1. Why were you initially drawn to social epistemology?

It is only in recent years that I have come to recognize that some of the
issues I have been pursuing at different times in my career count as social epistemology. You might describe me, if you like, as an anonymous
member of the social epistemology tribe.

The concerns that have drawn me into social epistemology derive
from concerns in social ontology. There are three major issues in social ontology. They turn respectively on the truth or falsity of what I
describe as individualism, atomism and singularism. The individualism
issue, which actually has few implications for epistemology, is whether
social life brings new forces or laws on stream that put constraints on
how individuals behave. Are there laws whose operation means that
individuals must behave in a manner that is not intelligible just on the
basis of an independent understanding of people's psychology and context? Anti-individualists argue that, yes, there are. This kind of doctrine
has traditionally been associated, rightly or wrongly, with Durkheim
and certain sociologists but it does not really raise questions in social
epistemology. For the record, I argue against it in my 1993 book *The
Common Mind*.

The other two issues in social ontology do raise epistemological issues and they have each engaged me greatly at different periods. The
first is the atomist question, as I call it, as to whether human beings
depend on interaction with one another — in particular, depend in more
than just a causal manner — for being able to display some of their distinctive, mental capacities. That question usually turns on the issue of
whether they depend on mutual interaction for the capacity to reason.
This is not the capacity just to transition rationally from certain beliefs
or intentions to other beliefs or intentions that they support, as many
non-human animals can certainly do. Just to take the belief case, it is

the capacity on people's part to recognize the truth of certain of their beliefs — to be able, when they believe that p, to think and believe of p that it is true — and to be able to form the belief that therefore it must be true that q, where 'p' entails 'q'". The access to thoughts such as 'therefore q' or 'so q' marks the divide between reasoning creatures like us and other creatures that do not reason, however rational they may be.

The atomist issue leads quickly into social epistemology, at least on the view that anti-atomism is true. When eighteenth century romantic authors like Rousseau and Herder began to argue that reasoning requires language and that language requires society, they opened up one of the largest issues in social epistemology: that of how it is that we can cooperate in the use of language, using it as a device for bootstrapping to the capacity for reasoning, without being able to reason in the first place. Those who followed their lead came under the formative influence of Hegel and developed the tradition of objective idealism in which the social achievement of a reasoning ability is hailed and celebrated but rarely subjected to what we nowadays would regards as searching analysis. I didn't ever sign up to that way of doing philosophy but from the earliest stages of my career I found the atomist question, and its implications for social epistemology, wholly engrossing. I developed anti-atomist views in a set of papers on Wittgenstein on rule-following and in the 1993 book, *The Common Mind*.

The third issue in social ontology I describe, in a term borrowed from Margaret Gilbert, as the singularist issue. This is the question as to whether the cooperation of human beings in the pursuit of more or less common goals — in particular, their cooperation in forming corporate entities that claim to be able to assume and honor obligations in the manner of individuals — ever leads to the appearance of groups that can count as agents in their own right. Singularists deny that cooperation ever leads to this result, arguing either that there are no group agents or that if there are, then they are reducible straightforwardly to individual agents: they are shadows cast by individuals, not entities that need to be posited in a full understanding of the social world. The divide between singularists and non-singularists opened up in the mid thirteenth century, soon after the Pope, Innocent IV, declared that while a corporate body — say, a university or a guild, a parish or a monastic order — might count as a *persona*, it could only count as a *persona ficta*. The theologians took the singularist side, casting such bodies as fictive persons without souls that could not be punished by anything like hell's fires. The lawyers took the anti-singularist side, casting them rather as artificial or legal persons and arguing that they could be held responsible in the law just like an individual person: they could enter contracts, for example, and sue and be sued for a breach. The antisingularism of these thinkers came back into fashion at the end of the nineteenth century, partly due to the work of the German historian, Otto Gierke. It was taken up with gusto by a number of English thinkers like the legal theorist, F.W. Maitland, the historian, J.N.Figgis, the guild socialist, G.D.H.Cole, and the political scientist, Harold Laski. The movement they established was very influential but tended to wither in the period leading up to the second world war; this may have been because of a mistaken association with fascist views on the organic nature of society and state.

Like the atomist issue, the singularist issue leads quickly into questions of social epistemology. If corporate bodies can count as agents in their own right, possessed of the attitudes that agency entails, then various epistemological questions arise. Are they themselves proper bearers of knowledge? Are they distinctive objects of inquiry on a par with individual subjects? And how do corporate and individual subjects relate to one another as the bearers of attitudes? How do individuals give life to the cognitive and other attitudes of the group agents in which they operate as members? I was interested in this issue, as in the other two issues, at the time of writing *The Common Mind* but I did not then have any particular base for arguing in favor of one side or the other, so that it did not figure in that book. It was only later, at the time of recognizing the discursive dilemma, that I began to see how it might be analytically addressed. And in a 2011 book, *Group Agency*, Christian List and I gave the question sustained attention.

2. What are your main contributions to the field of social epistemology?

'Contribution' is a factive term that implies success, perhaps even influence, and for that reason I am loathe to describe my work in such a presumptive way. But I am happy to give an account of my efforts on the two relevant fronts mentioned above: that is, in tackling the atomist and the singularist issues. I continue to stand broadly by the arguments defended in each area.

In attempting to argue against atomism, I developed a particular view of the rule-following problem that had been introduced by Wittgenstein and given a particularly clear — if not strictly Wittgensteinian — formulation in the work of Saul Kripke. If we human beings are to be able to reason, then we must be able to follow rules. And we must be able to follow rules that are so basic that they cannot themselves be articulated in other rules. We must be able to follow the rule, for example, that makes certain squiggly drawings into instances of an irregular figure, using such a finite base of examples to be able to cotton on to the rule and so to be able to put novel figures, more or less determinately, on either side of the regular-irregular divide. How do we do this? Certainly we each form a disposition in response to the examples to go on in a particular way. But if that is all that is involved in following the rule, then none of us could ever be mistaken about how the rule applies: the dispositional sourcing of response would leave no room for such a possibility.

What I argued in reply to this problem, very briefly and roughly, is that there are two aspects to our performance that makes the capacity for rule-following less than wholly mysterious. First, the disposition we form in response to examples has a cognitive aspect, enabling the examples to exemplify a more general pattern to which we can form the intention of remaining faithful as we seek to put novel figures on either side of the regular-irregular divide. We have a proleptic or jump-ahead grasp on that pattern, based in our confidence that as novel figures present themselves, our disposition will guide us on whether or not they are instances of the pattern: that pattern, as we can think of it ostensively, that the examples make salient. This is like the grasp I have on the route across Central Park from the Natural History Museum to the Metropolitan Museum. I could not draw that route or even give instructions for following it. But I can intend to follow that route, being confident that at each of a range of landmarks I will be disposed to go in the right direction to the next.

This aspect our performance in following basic rules still leaves in play the question as to how we could ever think of ourselves as being likely to be mistaken in reading such a rule: in extrapolating from examples to determine whether a novel figure is or is not irregular. The second aspect of our performance is meant to resolve that problem. As we identify the pattern that we intend to remain faithful to, we enfranchise or authorize others in determining exactly what that pattern is. We do not think reflectively to ourselves: the right pattern is the one that shows up in others' responses as well as our own. But we carry on as if we had that thought. Thus whenever we find that our extrapolation takes us in a different direction from that taken by some other person, we assume that something is going wrong on one or the other side. We balk at extrapolating confidently, looking for a special factor that can be taken to explain away either our own or the other's response, providing the best explanation of the discrepancy between us. Adjusting appropriately to that discovery, we carry on as before; or failing to agree on a common explanation, we may each continue on our own paths, confident that it is the other who is misled. Whatever path we eventually take, the effect of our practice is to warrant the philosophical comment that in basic rule-following we rely on one another to give ourselves patterns to which we can hope to remain faithful, while each being able to think that it is always possible to go wrong.

This line on rule-following and reasoning suggests that we are social creatures, not just in depending on one another for achieving many of our personal, practical goals, but also in depending on one another for the epistemological capacity to reason. The message is that there is no reasoning without co-reasoning, no access to patterns in the objective world that is not essentially intersubjective. Or in a slogan, no personal insight without social triangulation.

As the argument against atomism has taken me into social epistemology, so the argument against singularism has pushed me in the same direction. When I learned from the law and economics literature about the doctrinal paradox in the late 1990's, I immediately saw a reason for thinking that any form of singularism is false, generalizing from that paradox to a problem I described as the discursive dilemma. This problem suggested that in order to begin to function like a natural person, incorporating as a group agent, a collection of individuals has to be prepared to form attitudes binding on how members behave in the name of the group but that these attitudes cannot be a majoritarian function of the personal attitudes of the members themselves. And then Christian List and I proved a theorem which shows that a similar problem arises for any systematic method of deriving each of the attitudes of a group from the attitudes of members on the same proposition.

The impossibility theorem we established, bolstered by the various theorems that have followed it in the literature on judgment aggregation, reveals that there is a deep tension between two families of constraints on any group that seeks, as a group agent has to seek, to be able to perform like an individual person, in particular to be able to form, act on, and commit itself interpersonally to a certain set of attitudes. The first sort of constraint requires the group to be responsive to the attitudes of its members in the attitudes it forms; a group that was not so responsive could hardly expect members to go along reliably with its judgments, decisions and commitments. The second sort of constraint requires the group to form attitudes that satisfy a batch of rationality constraints, or at least to be able to satisfy them under challenge; a group that was unable to do this would not be an agent with which others could do business and would find itself pointed in different directions by conflicting attitudes.

The impossibility of satisfying such constraints at once is illustrated by the discursive dilemma in which three members of a would-be group agent, A, B and C, try to form the group beliefs on whether p, whether q, and whether p-and-q by majority voting. A and B may vote for 'p', C, against, committing the group to the belief that p. A and C may for 'q', B against, committing the group to the belief that q. But if they are individually consistent, A will vote for 'p-and-q', B and C will vote against, committing the group to the belief that not p-and-q. And so the group will have to face the dilemma either of giving up on the individual responsiveness ensured by majority voting or of giving up on collective rationality. But if it is to form a group agent, it cannot give up on rationality. Thus it has to decide to form attitudes that on some proposition are not a majoritarian function of the attitudes of members. It might decide, for example, that as a group it should endorse the belief that p, that q and, despite the lack of personal support, that p-and-q.

The discontinuity between group-level and individual-level attitudes in a group agent means that it is plausible to think of such a corporate body as a center of attitude and action with its own integrity: a body that cannot be properly understood just by focusing on the individual agents who make it up. And once we take that view of group agency, then a host of issues arises in social epistemology. Are group agents centers of knowledge? Can they be organized so as to increase their reliability: their ability to track the truth reliably in the beliefs they form as well as their ability to form beliefs that are reliable indicators of the truth; for short, their epistemic sensitivity and safety? How much knowledge of overall group attitudes is required among the members for the group to be able to perform satisfactorily? And how can individuals hold in mind at once both the attitudes they individually endorse and the attitudes they enact in the name of the group? Many such questions are opened up by the various chapters in Group Agency, though of the two of us Christian List is more likely to pursue them fruitfully in his further work; he has much greater command of the formal techniquest required for dealing with a number of them.

3. What is the proper role of social epistemology in relation to other disciplines?

I think that the two discussions I mentioned, bearing on rule-following and group agency, each supports lessons for the social sciences and in that sense gives a role to social epistemology in relation to those disciplines. I will mention one lesson of this kind in each case. Something similar holds in relation to normative disciplines like ethics, politics and jurisprudence, as I shall indicate later.

The position I take on social atomism directs us to a very distinctive role for the understanding that people have of one another as co-followers of rules and, more generally, as creatures who are essentially co-reasoners. When I understand another person I do not merely bring their behavior under certain familiar causal laws, as I do when I understand a sequence of events in nature. Nor do I merely grasp that the behavior is rationally required as I do when I see that an animal does something because of the desire it has and the beliefs that its environment elicits as to how to satisfy that desire. I understand another person insofar as I see them as conversable: that is, as a partner with whom I know how I could enter conversation — were that possible, as it may not often be. I have a good sense of what they hold and seek, of how they might be challenged and changed, and of where they are subject to what I see as blind spots or no-go areas. Once we see the fundamental importance of this sort of understanding — it answers perhaps to received notions of *Verstehen* as distinct from *Erklaeren* — we recognize that it is often actually practiced in some forms of social science and that even when it is not practiced, it ought to represent a constraint on the social-scientific explanations we endorse, as indeed Max Weber argued. We are entitled to expect of any supposed regularity in the social domain, however well supported by statistical or other evidence, that we can make conversable sense of how people must act if the regularity is to be reliably sustained.

The group agency discussion has an important lesson for the social sciences as well. This is that it makes very good sense, contrary to what some methodologists argue, to treat group agents as agents in their own right, seeking to make sense of them at the group level. The lesson applies to bodies like the firms that economists study, the governments that figure in political science, and the states that are treated as sovereign agents in the field of international relations. There may be a place for looking within such a group in order to identify the sources of certain effects — for example, certain failures of corporate rationality. But if the members are disposed and organized to cooperate in maintaining an intelligible, indeed a conversable profile for the body as a whole, and if the adjustments whereby they do this can be extremely complex and opaque — even to the members themselves — then the best understanding available of the performance of the group may be to have a good sense of its more secure goals and of its capacity to respond flexibly to evidence and opportunity in its pursuit of those goals. This involves treating the group agent as a black box, abstracting from the internal maneuverings of members, but for many epistemic purposes that may be heuristically indispensable.

The two areas of discussion mentioned support lessons also for normative rather than empirical projects. Thus the focus on conversability that the rule-following discussion supports argues for a broadly epistemological version of the ideal of respect that figures in so many theories. To relate as a co-reasoner with someone is to seek influence over the person but always in the exercise of offering take-it-or-leave-it reasons. This suggests that that sort of treatment has a natural priority in interpersonal dealings and it allows us to give a plausible account of respect. To respect someone under that account will be to abjure any

form of influence — say, by force or coercion, deception or manipula-
tion — that is inconsistent with such co-reasoning.

The discussion of group agency has even sharper normative implications. It suggests that in the domain of behavior that is allowed to any
corporate agent — in the domain where it is given the right to take one
or another course of action — that agent ought to be held responsible
in its own right for what it does there. Whatever it does will be done
by individuals and they may be blameworthy for playing a part that
they could have refused to play. But at the same time that they are held
responsible for their discretionary roles, the corporate entity as a whole
can be held responsible for allowing, perhaps even planning, for the
actions taken. This is particularly important, since there are many cases,
especially on the theory of group agency discussed, where the individuals who do ill in the name of a group may have bona fide excuses of
ignorance or pressure for behaving as they did, so that if the group as
a whole is not held responsible then there may be a normatively objec-
tionable deficit of accounting and regulation. There are many examples
that illustrate the point. One is the sinking of a ferry, the Herald of Free
Enterprise, in Zeebrugge in 1989. Although a British government report
castigated the company in charge for its widespread, long-lived slop-
piness and negligence, the courts refused to hold it criminally liable, on
the grounds that no individual in particular could be treated as liable in
a suitable degree.

4. What have been the most significant advances in social epistemology?

Although I am admirer of the work done in the area, particularly the
work of Alvin Goldman and his associates, I am too much of an outsi-
der — too much of an anonymous member of the confraternity — to be
able to speak with any authority on this question.

5. What are the most important open problems in social epistemology and what are the prospects for progress?

Again, it would be presumptious of me to address this issue in an overall manner. I can only say that in the field of group agency, I see many
open questions for social epistemology. These mainly concern the institutional designs whereby groups can be best organized for the production, dissemination and preservation of knowledge. Christian List and I
point to a range of such issues in Part II of *Group Agency*.

15

Erik J. Olsson

Professor of Philosophy
Lund University, Sweden

---

1. Why were you initially drawn to social epistemology?

My original interest was in epistemology in the traditional individualistic sense. This led me to study the concept of epistemic coherence, the property which beliefs have when they in some sense "hang well together", a topic which I wrote my dissertation on (Olsson, 1997). In the dissertation I studied coherence from the point of view of theories of belief revision, which was a hot topic at the time. Belief revision was then synonymous with the AGM theory of Alchourrón, Gärdenfors and Makinson, and its variants. In the AGM theory, belief revision is studied from a logical point of view, and the resources available are basically sentential logic plus set theory. A belief state is represented as a set of sentences or set of possible worlds together with some way of representing the notion that different beliefs can be more or less firmly held (more or less "entrenched") in a given belief system. Consequently, the resources available for capturing the concept of coherence were quite limited. In particular, I sensed a lack of a notion of "evidential independence": the idea that two or more pieces of evidence originated from independent sources. I thought that coherence has epistemic force only if the items that cohere had some degree of evidential independence.

After my PhD, I turned to probability theory as a framework for studying coherence. It turned out that this was a good move because I discovered, much to my delight, that the missing notion of independence could actually be captured in probabilistic terms, namely as a form of conditional independence. My first influence came from a paper by Peter Klein and Ted Warfield in *Analysis* where they presented a probabilistic argument to the effect that coherence cannot be truth conducive (Klein and Warfield, 1994). Their argument was that a set of observations can often be expanded with an explanation. Such an expanded set is more coherent, from an explanatory point of view, than the original smaller set. But, unless the explanation follows from the observations (which would an unusual case), the new set will be less likely to be true as a whole than the original. Hence, coherence is not truth conducive. However, I thought there was something fishy with this argument. The inquiry that followed led me to study C. I. Lewis's work on coherence in his book from 1946. One interesting fact about Lewis – and this is where social epistemology enters the picture – is that he takes a case of several reporters or witnesses reporting the same story as the paradigm case of coherence. Thus, he departs from the traditional view that coherence is prototypically a property of an individual inquirer's beliefs. However, Lewis grants of course that we can also apply the concept of coherence to individual beliefs or memories (his main application in the end). Those beliefs or memories are then seen as analogous to separate witness testimonies in court. This idea of Lewis's opened up the possibility of studying witness scenarios on an abstract probabilistic level and applying the findings to the traditional problems of epistemology, mostly skepticism, in which the concept of coherence has been traditionally put to use. This I did in my later work on coherence, which culminated in my book *Against Coherence* (Olsson, 2005). I return to the arguments of this book below.

My more recent work on social epistemology was inspired mainly by two sources. One was the Hegselmann-Krause simulation model of collective inquiry, especially their 2006 paper, and the other Alvin I. Goldman's theory of what he calls veritistic social epistemology, as laid out with characteristic scholarly excellence in his *Knowledge in a Social World* from 1999. My own contribution can be seen as an attempt to combine these two approaches into one or, more precisely, to devise a simulation model of inquiry which would, in the spirit of Goldman, use Bayesian updating and allow for the epistemic value of social practices to be objectively assessed. Let me explain.

In their 2006 paper, Hegselmann and Krause, inspired by Lehrer and Wagner (1981), proposed a non-Bayesian model for determining the chances for the truth to be found and broadly accepted in situations in which only some inquirers are reliable. The communication process was taken to consist in a mutual exchange of opinions between all individuals, reliable or not. H&K assume – intriguingly – that there is a true opinion, T, in the space of possible opinions that may be capable of "attracting" individuals to various degrees. An interesting result that came out of their work was that even if only some of the individuals are reliable, the group will gradually approach a consensus position which is close to the truth, although it may not be the exact truth. However, the model does not take into consideration the group members' assessment of the reliability of the other members, although that assessment is bound to be important in the overall persuasive effect of a deliberative contribution (e.g. an argument or the statement of an opinion).

The model, moreover, is based on a linear method for updating opinions that seems to lack independent standing in the philosophical literature. Having read Hegselmann and Krause's paper, I thought the model could be improved in these regards. In particular, I thought that a more convincing model would allow for the inclusion of trust as a factor in the updating process and that standard Bayesian updating would be an improvement upon the updating rule actually used. As I recall it, this was the first motivation for us – Staffan Angere who was a PhD student at the time and I – to start working on a Bayesian simulation model of social networks. See Olsson (2008) for a critical overview of the Hegselmann-Krause model.

The second motivation came from Goldman's work in social epistemology. In his 1999 book, Goldman outlines a theory for how to evaluate social practices with respect to their "veritistic value", i.e., their tendency to promote the acquisition of true beliefs (and impede the acquisition of false beliefs) in society. Goldman's main proposal is that degrees of belief (DB) have veritistic value relative to a question Q, so that any DB in the true answer to Q has the same amount of V-value as the strength of the DB. In Goldman's terminology, V-value of $DB_X(true) = X$. Suppose, for example, that Mary is interested in the question whether it will rain tomorrow. If the strength of Mary's belief that it will rain tomorrow is .8, and it will in fact rain tomorrow, then the V-value of Mary's state of belief vis-à-vis the rain issue is .8. This idea is then extended to cover social practices, e.g. relying on experts, trusting one another, etc. Goldman's main proposal in this regard is that the veritistic value of a practice can be computed as the average over the veritistic values of all applications of the practice. In the same work, Goldman raises a number of serious worries for his account. Two of them concern the possibility of determining the veritistic value of a practice in a concrete case because (1) we often don't know what beliefs are actually true, and (2) even if we did, the task of determining the veritistic value would be computationally extremely difficult. Thus the second goal we set ourselves when developing our Bayesian simulator was that it should be able ₜo compute veritistic values of interesting social practices automatically, thus solving Goldman's computational problem, at least in principle.

2. What are your main contributions to the field of social epistemology?

My main early contribution to social epistemology was my inquiry into coherence in a probabilistic setting, taking Lewis's witness scenario as a paradigm case. As I explained, the book, and the papers upon which it was based, combined individualistic and social epistemology in one philosophical inquiry. I argued, for instance, that while Klein and War-field's argument against the coherence theory was flawed, a version of their conclusion could actually be shown to hold. It could be shown that coherence, properly understood, is not truth conducive in the following sense: there is no measure of coherence such that a higher degree of coherence is positively correlated with a higher posterior probability that the statements in the set are true (i.e. given that they have been reported by witnesses or, analogously, form the contents of a given subject's beliefs). I have continued to write on coherence and witness agreement, although less intensely than I used to. For a recent example on the role of witness coherence and reliability in law see Schubert and Olsson (2012).

My recent work has focused on developing our Bayesian simulator and applying it to various issues in social epistemology. As for the first project, my role has often been to suggest various changes and additions to the simulator. These proposals have then been implemented by Angere, who is not only an outstanding philosopher and mathematician but also an excellent computer programmer, a rare and valuable combination of talents. Angere came up with the basic underlying Bayesian model, Laputa, and has made numerous changes and improvements to the simulator in the course of its history. He is mostly to be credited for the simulator bearing the same name, whereas my main contribution – apart from suggesting revisions and additions – has been to find interesting applications. I should mentioned that the way in which Laputa treats trust: as a second order probability or, more precisely, a credence in objective reliability, is reminiscent of how I conceived of witness reliability in my later work on coherence.

I see Laputa as my main contribution to social epistemology so far, and since I am still excited about it I have decided to include some details about the simulation framework (based on the exposition in Olsson 2011). The reader is advised to consult Vallinder and Olsson (2012) regarding the underlying probabilistic model. The model was originally laid out in Angere (manuscript), but at the moment of writing this paper is still unpublished.

A basic notion in Laputa is that of a *social network* in which people can communicate with each other. Social networks are represented as graphs in which the nodes represent inquirers and the links represent communication channels. The links are directed, allowing for one-way communication. Figure 1 is an example.

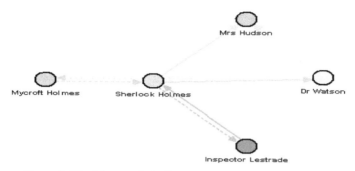

Figure 1: The (characteristically exclusive) social network of Sherlock
Holmes as represented in Laputa.

Following Goldman, it is assumed that all inquirers focus on answering
one and the same question: whether p or not-p. For example, p can be
the proposition "The economic crises will soon be over". The *initial
degree of belief* is an inquirer's credence (subjective probability) in p
from the start. *Inquiry accuracy* is the reliability of the inquirer's own
inquiries. The *inquiry chance* is the probability that the inquirer will
conduct an inquiry. The *inquiry trust* is the inquirer's degree of "self-
trust", i.e., her degree of trust in her own inquiries. Likewise, there are
a number of parameters for each link. The *communication chance* is the
probability that the sender will send a message given that her degree of
belief exceeds the *threshold of assertion*. As for the latter, if the threshold is set at .90, this means that the sender needs to believe p (not-p)
to a degree .90 in order for her to "assert" p (not-p) in the network. The
listen trust is the recipients trust in the sender.

Running Laputa can mean to construct a network such as that in Figure 1, assign initial values to the inquirer and link parameters, and then
click on a "run" button. This triggers Laputa to run through a series
of steps, each step representing a chance for an inquirer to conduct an
inquiry, to communicate (send, listen) to the other inquirers to which
she is connected, or to do both. After each step, Laputa will update the
whole network according to the information received by the inquirers.
This is done in accordance with standard Bayesian techniques. Thus,
a new degree of belief is computed for each inquirer based on the old
degree of belief and the new information received through inquiry and/
or listening to other inquirers. Laputa also updates the inquiry trust and
listen trust parameters in accordance with Bayesian principles. After
such a process of network updating, Laputa computes the veristic value
of the "network evoluation" as the difference between the average final

and initial degrees of belief. A positive value means that there was an increase in veritistic value: the process of inquiry and communication brought people somewhat closer to the truth, at least on the average.

However, the veritistic value of a particular *network evolution* is perhaps not so interesting. What we would like to do is to assess the veritistic value of a *practice*. The first thing to note is that what we have learned about Laputa so far allows us to study the V-value of a particular *application* of a practice. Consider for instance the practice of trusting other people. Before we run the network we can adjust the listen trust parameter for all the links so that this condition is satisfied. Now we run the network as previously described, preferably until the network stabilizes and relatively fixed degrees of belief have been obtained. What we get as a result is the V-value of the practice of trusting other people as applied to the particular network at hand and its initial state (e.g. the Sherlock Holmes network of Figure 1).

Laputa now solves the problem of computing the veritistic value of a practice as an average over the veritistic values of all its (considered) applications. It does so by allowing its user to specify various features or "desiderata" of networks at an abstract level. The program can then randomly generate a large number of networks, of different sizes, having those features, letting them evolve, collecting the corresponding V-values and, finally, outputting the average V-value of all the network evolutions it has examined. This allows Laputa to compute the V-value of a large number of interesting practices. For instance, Laputa can be told, at the abstract level, to study 10,000 randomly generated networks in which inquirers trust each other to a certain degree. The resulting V-value is a measure of the V-value of the practice of trusting other people to that degree, independently of any particular network. All this is done in Laputa's "batch window". Further details about how this works can be found in Olsson (2011).

Apart from allowing the veritistic value of practices to be determined, the development of Laputa had two conceptual bonuses that should be highlighted. First, Laputa can differentiate between the short run and long run veritistic performance of a practice. Suppose for example that we want to know how beneficial truth telling is in the long run. This problem could be studied by setting the number of steps per trial to, say, 100. If we are more interested in short term uses, we could instead set the number of steps to a smaller number, say, 5 or 10.

Secondly, Laputa can help us to get clearer on what a social practice is. From the point of view of Laputa, a social practices can be identified with a *network constraint*. Any such constraint which can be imposed in Laputa's batch window can be studied from the point of view of veristitic value in the manner just described. This includes constraints that would perhaps not normally be described as social practices, e.g., "being reliable in one's inquiries to degree .75". Nevertheless, identifying a social practice with a network constraint may still be a fruitful *explication* of the concept of a social practice, in the sense of Carnap (1950). Laputa can be downloaded for free from *http://www.luiq.lu.se/portfolio-item/laputa/*

The model was proposed first and foremost as a *normative* model of group deliberation and communication. Nevertheless, it has been argued that group communication in Laputa exhibits a number of characteristics of real life group communication, including polarization, i.e. the process whereby "members of a deliberating group predictably move toward a more extreme point in the direction indicated by the members' predeliberation tendencies" (Sunstein, 2002). For this point see Olsson (2013) and, for a study of the role of overconfidence, Vallinder and Olsson (2014). Laputa has been applied to a number of different philosophical issues. It is applied to Goldman's computational problem in Olsson (2011). It is applied to the problem of norms of assertion in epistemology in Olsson and Vallinder (2013), inspired by the account in Douven (2006). And It is applied to the Argument from Disagreement in ethics in Vallinder and Olsson (2013).

3. What is the proper role of social epistemology in relation to other disciplines?

This is obviously a huge subject. I will confine myself to just one aspect of it: the relation between social epistemology and traditional epistemology. The background is Alvin Goldman's view that social epistemology should be assimilated to epistemology in the traditional sense because social epistemology is, as he puts it, "real epistemology" (Goldman, 2010). I am inclined to question this view. Obviously, this is not in any way a dismissal of social epistemology as such. It is only a claim that the two – social and traditional individualistic epistemology – are different disciplines and should, at least for the time being, be viewed as such.

In his paper, Goldman surveys a number of issues in social epistemology that are introduced roughly in order of increasing degree of "sociality". For starters, testimony and peer disagreement are certainly social phenomena, although they are so in a comparatively innocent sense. Here the focus is still on the individual. It is just that her individual inquiry is placed in a wider social context. The next step up the social ladder is to study institutions with respect to how good they serve the epistemic purposes of individuals that aspire to attain truth and avoid falsehood. This step is significant because it represents a shift of attention from the individual person to the social institution and its design.

We can proceed still further. Several researchers have maintained that it makes good sense to ascribe knowledge, belief, acceptance and the like not only to individuals but also to groups. Goldman is open to this suggestion, pointing out that it would raise interesting issues of how individual judgments are aggregated to form collective ones.

Now Goldman thinks that we can ascend up this social ladder and still do epistemology in the traditional sense, at least so long as there is continuity with what he takes to be the *core assumptions* of traditional epistemology, such as the objectivity of truth and the central role of normativity and rationality. Let us refer to this requirement as that of *individual-to-social continuity*. A further criterion that he introduces is that the social phenomena we are considering, like the Internet or judicial tribunals, should have causal influence on individual inquirer's doxastic attitudes. I will call this condition that of *social-to-individual causality*.

Let me now turn to my first critical point. Goldman, as I just mentioned, favors a characterization of epistemology in terms of certain "core assumptions". I agree that there is, on this characterization, much continuity between Goldman style social epistemology and traditional epistemology. After all, this brand of social epistemology is a normative enterprise; and it is predicated on the assumption of truth being an objective, largely mind-independent, affair, and so on for several other core ideas.

What I want to suggest, however, is that the picture changes if we, as indeed I believe many practitioners do, think of traditional epistemology, not or at least not only in terms a set of core assumption but also in terms of a set of *core issues*. If we do, the case for including much of social epistemology in traditional epistemology seems less compelling. Let me try to explain why.

What are the core issues in traditional epistemology? Well, the problem of skepticism would certainly be one, as would the problem of accounting for the nature of knowledge. And then we have or course the traditional rationalist-empiricist debate concerning the identification of legitimate *sources* of knowledge. We shouldn't forget the value problem: why is knowledge distinctively valuable? Then there is the question regarding the *limits* of knowledge. Are there truths that cannot be known? This list of core issues could of course be extended.

Now it seems far from obvious that social epistemology has much to offer by way of answering these and other core issues of traditional epistemology. The problem of the nature of knowledge, for instance, does not seem to involve in any crucial way a social dimension. Neither does the problem of the limits of knowledge. At least this is what I anticipate that most mainstream researchers would say about these cases. (I will return to social accounts of the core issues at the end of this remark.) So, Goldman's argument for his main thesis depends in large measure on a characterization of traditional epistemology that I believe many mainstream epistemologists would find seriously incomplete. I take this claim of mine to be in accord with a standard Kuhnian view on what constitutes a research paradigm, where the core issues – the questions that are considered to be most urgent – play a pivotal role for that purpose.

My second point will be that Goldman's argument seems to prove too much. My reasons for this claim draws on an analogy with the social sciences. The science of psychology is defined in Encyclopedia Britannica as a "scientific discipline that studies mental processes in humans and other animals". There we also learn that "the issues studied by psychologists cover a wide spectrum, comprising learning, cognition, intelligence, motivation, emotion, perception, personality, mental disorders, and the study of the extent to which individual differences are inherited or are shaped environmentally". Sociology, on the other hand, is claimed to be "a social science that studies human societies, their interactions, and the processes that preserve and change them". Furthermore, "it does this by examining the dynamics of constituent parts of societies such as institutions, communities, populations, and gender, racial, or age groups". Finally, "sociology also studies social status or stratification, social movements, and social change, as well as societal disorders in the form of crime, deviance, and revolution".

Now clearly, there is, on this description, much continuity between psychology and sociology so that, to quote from the same source, "[t]he broad nature of sociology causes it to overlap with other social sciences such as ... psychology". For instance, both aim at accounting for various aspects of human behavior, including various forms of "disorder". Moreover, the groups studied by sociology causally influence the behavior of the individuals studied by psychology. Indeed, it is according to this authoritative source "sociology's task to discover how organizations affect the behavior of persons".

On an abstract level, then, we have both individual-to-social continuity and social-to-individual causality. If Goldman were right in thinking that these very features are those that justify assimilating the social to the individual, sociology should be considered real psychology. But, as we know, it isn't.

The third point, or rather a question, is: what does it take for the social to be assimilated to the individual? The answer to this question, I believe, lies not or at least not only in individual-to-social continuity and social-to-individual causality. For the social to be assimilated to the individual, there has to be, I submit, a general feeling that the core issues in the individual domain cannot be satisfactorily dealt with, not even in approximation, without bringing in the corresponding social dimension. In a word, there has to be a general sense of *anomaly* in the individual domain. The assimilation of social psychology to psychology bears witness to the fact that some issues in psychology are indeed such that they cannot be even be approximately accounted for from a purely individual perspective.

A parallel case in epistemology is its relatively recent assimilation of a theory of testimony. The inclusion of testimony in mainstream epistemology is due to the fact that, thanks mainly to C. A. J. Coady (1992) and his followers, it has become increasingly clear that the traditional account of the sources of knowledge in terms of perception, memory, intuition, and so on, is utterly incomplete. Unless we take testimony to be a full-fledged source of knowledge, we must conclude that we have much less knowledge than we thought we had. In this way, the traditional problem of accounting for the sources of knowledge simply could not be solved without bringing in, as a last resort, some social machinery.

It follows that for social epistemology *as a whole* to become a legitimate extension of traditional epistemology, it must be shown to have crucial bearing on a substantial number of core issues in the individual domain. *Pace* Goldman, it doesn't suffice that it complies with most of the core assumptions.

Here is how the current situation looks to me: Traditional epistemology and social epistemology are different areas of philosophical inquiry defined partly by their different sets of core issues. However, they share an interest in the epistemology of testimony which may, for reasons already given, be legitimately viewed as real traditional epistemology. Maybe the same is true also of the epistemology of disagreement without which, it could be maintained, any theory of justification would be radically incomplete, although I am less sure in that case. At any rate, once we have accepted the epistemology of testimony as real epistemology, it can also be invoked to shed light on another traditional issue, the value of knowledge. Clearly, knowledge is valuable in part because it gives the person who has it the right to transmit it to others via the speech act of sincere assertion or testimony. Having such a right is a good thing. Surely, any theory of the value of knowledge would, in the end, need to accommodate this social observation. So testimony is special in the sense that it is intimately tied to two fundamental problems of mainstream epistemology. Small wonder that it could be assimilated without much protest! Yet apart from these central problems concerning the sources and value of knowledge, respectively, there is to my mind no clear further candidate for socialization among the traditional core issues. So, as things stand, I am afraid that I do not fully share Goldman's optimisms regarding the prospects of a more far-reaching inclusion of social epistemology within epistemology as traditionally conceived. Social epistemology is valuable and it is so largely independently of the core issues of traditional epistemology.

4. What have been the most significant advances in social epistemology?

I should say at the beginning that, coming to social epistemology rather late, I lack a comprehensive overview of the now rather extensive field. The following remarks will have to be rather impressionistic, I am afraid. At any rate, I tend to think of the "veritistic" contributions to social epistemology as the most important ones. By that I mean the kind of social epistemology in which a robust notion of truth plays a major role. I am thinking, for instance, of Nicolas de Condorcet's early jury theorem. Condorcet considered a case of assembly members voting independently on a proposition p, e.g. the proposition that the accused is guilty. He assumed, furthermore, that the voters are at least somewhat reliable and that they are reliable to the same degree, r (e.g. r = 0.6). He then showed that the probability that the majority is correct exceeds r and, moreover, that this probability converges to 1 as the number of voters goes to infinity. In other words, the view of the majority is more likely to be correct than the view of an individual voter, and the greater the number of voters, the more reliable is the voice of the majority. There have been important recent extensions of and elaborations on these results by Christian List, Robert E. Goodin and others (e.g. List and Goodin 2001, Goodin 2003). I take the study of coherence, as I have described it above, to be mainly a further extension of Condorcet's pioneering work. It extends Condorcet's work e.g. by allowing witnesses to be in less than full agreement. The basic model studied involves independent but somewhat reliable witnesses giving coherent reports, and the question is whether a report set which is more coherent (or exhibiting greater agreement) is thereby more likely to be true *ceteris paribus*. Apart from work already mentioned, Luc Bovens and Stephan Hartmann's 2003 book *Bayesian Epistemology* is a major contribution to this field.

A second branch of veritistic social epistemology considers social practices more generally (and with less mathematical rigor), including free speech. The first major work in this area is generally taken to be John Stuart Mill's famous treatise *On Liberty*, which provides a systematic and still influential defense of free speech from the point of view of the value of truth. Goldman's aforementioned *Knowledge in a Social World* belongs, as I see it, to this second branch of veristic social epistemology. Chapter 7 of Goldman's book contains a thorough treatment of the subject.

The "new wave" in this area, from my perspective, is to use computer simulation techniques to study the, often very complex, relationship between various social practices and the dissemination and acquisition of true belief. As I mentioned, Hegselmann and Krause has done seminal work in this field, drawing on Lehrer and Wagner (1981). It should be added that Lehrer and Wagner did not actually study belief convergence from a veritistic point of view. Truth plays no role in their model. Hegselmann and Krause should be credited for bringing truth into the picture. Rainer Hegselmann has continued to do important work in this field, as have, for instance, Igor Douven (2010) and Kevin Zollmann (2007), who was inspired by Bala and Goyal (1998). For instance, Douven has applied a Hegselmann-Krause style model in an enlightening way to the debate over disagreement in mainstream epistemology. Douven and Kelp (2011) is a useful overview of recent work on computer-aided social epistemology.

5. What are the most important open problems in social epistemology and what are the prospects for progress?

There are a surprising number of societal issues that are important but which do not seem to fall into any particular established discipline. On closer examination, these issues may turn out to be of a social-epistemological kind. One example, among many, is how to evaluate and possibly improve judicial procedures. We obviously want judicial procedures to end in true judgments, so that the accused is sentenced if and only if he or she is actually guilty. What seems to have happened in many countries is that a judicial system has evolved over the years in a trial and error fashion with little or no systematic oversight of the judiciary as a whole. One example is the problem of jury size. How many jurors should be involved in a trial? This is a strikingly simple question but if one look at different countries, one tends to get very different answers. In Sweden, there are four jurors participating in a district court trial. In the US and the UK, there are usually 12 jurors. In Scotland, the number is 15, and so on. Curiously, few legal scholars seems to know the reason why a particular number was adopted. The likely reply is "because this is the way it has always been".

So, is there such a unique number from an epistemological point of view? If social epistemology could have something to say on this issue, this could be hugely beneficial because nobody else seems to be in a position to address it. This said, there is useful work in organizational and experimental psychology that may be relevant. To add to the (local) urgency of this matter: in Sweden there seems to be a developing consensus, judging by the debate in the public domain, that the judicial system, or a substantial part of it, is in need of revision. For example, in a recent (unscientific) poll most professional Swedish judges expressed their dissatisfaction with the layman jury system ("nämndemannasyste-met"). Yet, there is no consensus regarding who should be revising it, or what information should be brought to bear on that decision. I am not saying, or course, that social epistemologist should be taking over the revision of the judiciary. However, I do think that some of the things we are doing can be relevant in such a process.

One of the more recent Laputa studies addresses the problem of assessing the optimal number of jurors in a trial (Angere, Olsson and Genot, in press). Our preliminary results support the Scottish 15 juror system. While adding another juror always adds epistemic value, there is a diminishing marginal return, and beyond 15 jurors there is little surplus epistemic value to be had by adding one more. If one takes into account the administrative cost of adding another juror or the fact (well-known to organizational psychologists) that the size of the group tends to be negatively correlated with the efforts of its members, results may go in the direction of smaller juries.

I mention this in order to make a general point: This unpublished study somehow received unexpected attention in Swedish media (e.g. Lind, 2012). I do not take this to be an indication of the importance of the results, which are rudimentary at best. Rather I take it to be an indication that there is so little evidence to draw on in this area that any new results that have a touch of objectivity will be appreciated and discussed. Very likely, other simulation frameworks could provide valuable input here as well, and I encourage their practitioners to work on the problem. At any rate, here is an area where society is in great need of assistance and where social epistemologists seem to be sitting on, or being in the process of developing, some promising tools.

References

Angere, S. (manuscript), "Knowledge in a Social Network", http://lup.lub.lu.se/luur/download?func=downloadFile&recordOId=4393834&fileOId=4393835.

Angere, S., Olsson, E. J. and Genot, E. (in press), "Inquiry and Deliberation in Judicial Systems: the Problem of Jury Size", in: Baskent, C. (Ed.), *Interrogative Models of Inquiry: Developments in Inquiry and Questions*, Springer.

Bala, V., and Goyal, S. (1998), "Learning from Neighbours", *Review of Economic Studies Limited* 65: 595-621.

Bovens, L, and Hartmann, S. (2003), *Bayesian Epistemology*, Oxford: Oxford University Press.

Coady, C. A. J. (1992). *Testimony: A Philosophical Study*. Oxford: Clarendon Press.

Carnap, R. (1950), *Logical Foundations of Probability*, Chicago: University of Chicago Press.

Douven, Igor. (2006), "Assertion, Knowledge, and Rational Credibility", *Philosophical Review* 115 (4): 449-485.

Douven, I. (2010), "Simulating Peer Disagreements", *Studies in History and Philosophy of Science* 41: 148–157.

Douven, I., and Kelp, C. (2011), "Truth Approximation, Social Epistemology, and Opinion Dynamics, *Erkenntnis* 75: 271-283.

Goldman, A. I. (1999), *Knowledge in a Social World*, Oxford: Oxford University Press.

Goldman, A. I. (2010), "Why Social Epistemology is Real Epistemology", in Haddock, A., Millar, A., and Pritchard, D. (eds.), *Social Epistemology*, New York: Oxford University Press.

Goodin, R. E. (2003), *Reflective Democracy*, Oxford: Oxford University Press.

Hegselmann, R., and Krause, U. (2006), "Truth and Cognitive Division of Labour: First Steps Towards a Computer-Aided Social Epistemology", *Journal of Artificial Societies and Social Simulation* 9 (3).

Klein, P. and Warfield, T. A. (1994), "What Price Coherence?". *Analysis*, 54: 129-32.

Lehrer, K., and Wagner, C. G. (1981), *Rational consensus in science and society*, D. Reidel: Dordrecht.

Lewis, C. I. (1946), *An Analysis of Knowledge and Valuation*, LaSalle: Open Court.

Lind, A. (2012), "Stor jury ökar rättssäkerheten", *Jusektidningen* 2, p. 4.

List, C., and Goodin R. E. (2001), "Epistemic Democracy: Generalizing the Condorcet Jury Theorem", *Journal of Political Philosophy* 9: 277-306.

Olsson, E. J. (1997), *Coherence: Studies in Epistemology and Belief Revision*, doctoral dissertation, Department of Philosophy, Uppsala University.

Olsson, E. J. (2005), *Against Coherence: Truth, Probability, and Justification*, Oxford: Oxford University Press.

Olsson, E. J. (2008), "Knowledge, Truth, and Bullshit: Reflections on Frankfurt", *Midwest Studies in Philosophy* 32: 94-110.

Olsson, E. J. (2011), "A Simulation Approach to Veritistic Social Epistemology", *Episteme* 8 (2): 127-143.

Olsson, E. J. (2013), "A Bayesian Simulation Model of Group Deliberation and Polarization", in: Zenker, F. (Ed.), *Bayesian Argumentation: The Practical Side of Probability*, pp. 113-133.

Olsson, E. J., and Vallinder, A. (2013), "Norms of Assertion and Communication in Social Networks", *Synthese* 190: 2557-2571.

Schubert, S., and Olsson, E. J. (2012), "Coherence and Reliability in Judicial Reasoning", in Araszkiewicz, M. (ed.), *Artificial Intelligence, Coherence and Judicial Reasoning*, Springer Verlag.

Sunstein, C. R. (2002), "The Law of Group Polarization", *The Journal of Political Philosophy* 10 (2): 175-195.

Vallinder, A., and Olsson, E. J. (2013), "Do Computer Simulations Support the Argument from Disagreement?", *Synthese* 190: 1437-1454.

Vallinder, A., and Olsson, E. J. (2014), "Trust and the Value of Overconfidence: A Bayesian Perspective on Social Network Communication", *Synthese* 191: 1991-2007.

Zollman, K. J. (2007), "The Communication Structure of Epistemic Communities", *Philosophy of Science* 74 (5): 574-587.

16

Frederick F. Schmitt

Professor of Philosophy
Indiana University

---

1. Why were you initially drawn to social epistemology?

I began thinking about issues in social epistemology in the late nineteen seventies. Although the term "social epistemology" had already been used to refer to empirical investigations now regarded as relevant to social epistemology, no one had recognized a social field within epistemology, and discussions of the issues were rare. Of course no one had ever doubted that social conditions are materially necessary for knowledge and affect which propositions we know. Early in Greek philosophy, Heraclitus and Xenophanes had recognized that cultural surroundings affect imagination and thus facilitate or limit observations, conjectures, and discoveries. It was traditional to allow testimony as a source, even an autonomous source, of opinion or probability, as contrasted with knowledge or *scientia*. The erosion of the distinction between knowledge and probability in early modern times and the increasing dependence of science on testimony made pressing the question whether to assimilate testimony to perceptual observation or treat it as an autonomous source of knowledge—a question explicit in Reid. In the nineteenth century Peirce treated social conditions as making a more substantial contribution to knowledge.

In twentieth century epistemology, an antipsychologistic orientation to logic and probability carried in train an antipathy to the relevance of social conditions to knowledge. By the early nineteen seventies, the representation of social issues in epistemology had shrunk to the consideration of asymmetries between self-knowledge and the knowledge of other minds. A focus of epistemology was the egocentric question what I should believe, given my experience of the world—a question making skepticism an outcome difficult to avoid. Accessibility internalism was generally assumed to be true for justification, ruling out the relevance of social conditions for justification on the ground that we cannot tell them to hold by reflection alone.

In the wake of Quine's "Epistemology Naturalized," naturalistic, externalist, and reliabilist approaches to knowledge gained prominence. These implied the relevance of psychology to knowledge, and this implication made it inevitable to wonder whether social conditions might be similarly relevant. Alvin Goldman began to make this line of thinking explicit, and this was undoubtedly the most important stimulus to my entry into social epistemology. The major naturalistic approaches to epistemology have social analogues. One naturalistic approach treats knowledge as a natural kind, the character of which is revealed by examining nature, perhaps by examining the natural functions of cognitive states (an approach developed by Hilary Kornblith). Another naturalistic approach analyzes the concept of knowledge on the assumption that our employment of the concept has the function of enabling us to meet our needs as natural creatures (an approach employed by Nietzsche and to be found recently in Edward Craig's *Knowledge and the State of Nature*, Oxford: Clarendon, 1990). A third naturalistic approach argues that the conditions of knowledge are exhausted by features that are in some sense natural—psychological features or relations to objects in the subject's environment. There is a social analogue of each approach. Analogous to the first naturalistic approach, we treat knowledge as a phenomenon consisting of social relations (an approach exemplified by the Strong Programme in the sociology of scientific knowledge). Analogous to the second naturalistic approach, we analyze the concept of knowledge on the assumption that it functions in social life to meet our basic needs (again, exemplified by Craig's work). Analogous to the third naturalistic approach, we argue that the conditions of knowledge, whether metaphysically necessary conditions or conceptual conditions, include social elements. I began my interest in social epistemology by pursuing the third approach, but I have been attracted to the second approach as well.

Naturalism was not the only source of my early interest in social epistemology. The Strong Programme in the sociology of scientific knowledge, associated with the University of Edinburgh, was much in the news in the late seventies. Although my attitude toward it was critical, and I took little of substance from it, the enthusiasm of its proponents for a social study of knowledge was contagious, sparking a desire to see whether a social epistemology might be defensible. Work by cognitive psychologists—Daniel Kahneman, Amos Tversky, Richard Nisbett, and Lee Ross, among many others—uncovered deviations of human reasoning from Bayesian and other allegedly a priori epistemic norms proposed by philosophers, deviations induced by structural and procedural features of human cognition, rather than by interference from noncognitive mechanisms. Psychologists generally assumed that the proposed a priori norms were correct, but philosophers were left wondering whether these norms could be correct if humans are guaranteed to violate them by structural or procedural features of cognition. To the extent that philosophers found this suggestion compelling, they were forced to admit that epistemic norms are hostage to the outcome of empirical psychological investigation. The parallel suggestion for empirical social investigation was then unavoidable: results of empirical sociology or other social sciences could in principle show that humans are guaranteed by social structural or relational conditions to violate proposed allegedly a priori epistemic norms for individual subjects. To the extent that this suggestion is attractive, an epistemologist ought to attend to the best empirical social science in envisioning the human subject to which proposed epistemic norms for individual subjects are to apply.

Another inspiration for social epistemology was feminist philosophy. Feminist epistemology had yet to develop, but one slogan of feminist philosophy, "the personal is political," prompted the thought that, despite its apparent autonomy from the social, knowledge in the individual might really be social after all. Yet another inspiration for social epistemology was Thomas Kuhn's case that social circumstances affect paradigm shifts in science. Finally, Gilbert Harman contributed to the Gettier literature and to social epistemology simultaneously by arguing that social circumstances beyond a subject's ken can prevent the subject from knowing.

2. What are your main contributions to the field of social epistemology?

I have generally chosen my topics in social epistemology with an eye to the overarching question whether social conditions figure in the conceptually or metaphysically necessary conditions of knowledge or in some other sense constitute knowledge. I have focused on this matter for knowledge possessed by individuals. To speak more precisely, I have focused on whether social conditions figure in the conditions of individual *justified beliefs*, since (for a reason mentioned below) it is uncontroversial that social conditions figure in the conditions of individual knowledge. I have focused on the epistemology of *individual* cognition because a case that social conditions figure here would show that sociality is ineliminable even in the domain most likely to be free from social conditions. I have always been aware that such a case is difficult to make and unlikely to be conclusive. It has seemed worth trying to the make the case because its success would establish that individual and social epistemology are inseparable at the root—that social epistemology is not merely an adjunct to individual epistemology.

With these general points for guidance, I divide my contributions to social epistemology into these categories:

Testimony. I find two pivotal questions here. The first in the proper order of inquiry is whether *reductionism* holds. Is the justification conferred on a belief by its being based on testimony derived ultimately from nontestimonial justification? On an inductive reductionist account, a belief on testimony is ultimately justified on the basis of an induction from perceptual observation (or in some cases, a priori judgment) to the conclusion that the testimony is reliable. A very important argument against this account, first developed by C. A. J. Coady is that in the typical case of belief on testimony, the subject lacks a sufficient firsthand basis for believing that the testimony is reliable, so cannot ultimately be justified on the basis of nontestimonially justified beliefs. The subject has not made enough observations to support the conclusion of reliability in this way. This is a powerful argument. At the same time, there have been several efforts to defend the inductive reductionist account, or similar reductionist accounts, and we still lack a decisive argument against it. A second argument against the inductive reductionist account is that belief on expert testimony cannot be justified ultimately on a nontestimonial basis, since it is impossible for a subject who is not an expert on a topic to have a firsthand inductive justification for the reliability of expert testimony on the topic. I offered such an argument in "Justification, Sociality, and Autonomy' (*Synthese* 73, 1987: 43-85). I went on to allow that, even if we cannot escape irreducible reliance on experts and testifiers more generally, there is value in partial autonomy, i.e., relying on our own observations in partial support of beliefs about the reliability of testifiers.

A different reductionist approach to testimonial justification attributes this justification to the availability of what I call the parity argument. In Keith Lehrer's version of this approach, the parity argument takes the form: I am worth of my trust in what I believe; others are as worthy of my trust in what they believe as I am in what I believe; so others are worthy of my trust in what they believe. On the parity account, my testimonial beliefs are justified because this parity argument is available to me. In "Testimonial Justification: The Parity Argument" (*Studies in the History and Philosophy of Science* 33, 2002: 385-406), I criticized the parity account on the ground that I am not in a position to support the premises of the parity argument in a manner that could confer justification on my testimonial belief. At least, I am in no such position if I lack a sufficient inductive justification that the testimony is reliable.

These matters concern the first pivotal question, whether reductionism holds. Concluding that reductionism is mistaken leads one to a nonclassical view of justification (albeit one already endorsed by Reid in the eighteenth century), according to which belief on testimony is justified in a manner not derived from nontestimonial sources. The denial of reductionism is, however, compatible with the view that a belief on testimony is justified in virtue of satisfying a standard account of individual justification. For example, it is compatible with the view that a belief on testimony is justified because testimony, or even apparent testimony, is a reliable source of belief. (I consider diverse reliabilist foundations for testimonial justification in "Social Epistemology," in John Greco and Ernest Sosa, eds., *Blackwell Guide to Epistemology*, Oxford: Blackwell, 1999, pp. 354-82.) Again, it is compatible with the view that a belief on testimony is justified because testimony, or even apparent testimony, provides the subject with evidence for the proposition believed, since it indicates the truth of the testimonial proposition. Assuming that the arguments against reductionism are sound, combining the nonreductionist view of testimony as an autonomous source of justification with a reliabilist or evidentialist view of justification does have the interesting consequence of ruling out the internalist requirement on justification that the subject be able to justify the belief that the testimony is reliable or amounts to evidence. But the view that we can derive that testimony is a source of justification from reliabilism or evidentialism still leaves us with an account of testimonial justification, though a nonclassical account, straightforwardly derived from standard individual epistemology. Moreover, the account is so far only nominally social. It does not by itself treat actual testimony as conferring justification on the subject's belief in a way different from that in which merely apparent, even hallucinated testimony could confer justification on the subject's belief. Real and apparent testimony would count as the same source on a broad individuation of sources. And even if a belief can be justified only if the subject hears a real utterance of a testifier, it does not follow that the subject must bear to the testifier anything we would colloquially call a social relation. The nonreductionist view does not take us very far into the social domain. It is merely a necessary step toward a robustly social view of testimonial justification.

We come now to the second pivotal question about testimony: does justification by testimony sometimes occur in virtue of a social relation between the subject and the testifier? I take it to be uncontroversial that a subject *knows* a proposition on the basis of testimony only if the subject is actually socially related to a testifier. Of course this entailment is analytic if "testimony" in the target for analysis requires the real testimony of a testifier. But even waiving that basis for the entailment, and allowing that the term "testimony" ranges over all apparent testimony, the entailment still holds because of the steep requirements of knowledge. To be sure, the common view that a subject knows a proposition on the basis of testimony only if the testifier knows the proposition has been forcefully challenged (by Jennifer Lackey and Peter Graham). But as far as I am aware, no one has questioned that knowledge on testimony requires that the subject is socially related to a testifier and that the testimony has desirable epistemic properties (perhaps the property of expressing a proposition the testifier is in a position to know merely by believing it because the testifier is propositionally justified in believing it). This makes knowledge on testimony robustly social. It could well be that the requirement on the testifier (perhaps of being in a position to know) matters because restricting the term "knowledge" to such cases promotes caution in testifying and receiving testimony, given the strong requirements on being in a position to know and the power of withholding the term "knowledge" to rebuke a subject who presents himself or herself as knowing. However this may be, the fact that the requirement is uncontroversial led me to focus not on whether knowledge on testimony is robustly social, but, more adventurously, on whether justification on testimony is so. It is in fact not intuitive that a subject is justified on testimony only if socially related to a testifier. I nevertheless made a tentative case for the following qualified view along these lines: if being justified in a belief requires having a reason for the belief, and the subject is justified in a belief on testimony but lacks an ultimate nontestimonial basis for it, then the subject has a reason for the belief, and that reason is the testifier's reason for the belief ("Testimonial Justification and Transindividual Reasons," in Jennifer Lackey and Ernest Sosa, eds. *The Epistemology of Testimony*, Oxford: Clarendon, 2006, pp. 193-224). This view entails that if the arguments against reductionism are sound, justification on testimony sometimes requires that the subject is socially related to another thinker having a reason to believe the proposition asserted. On this view, testimonial justification is constituted in part by actual social relations in certain circumstances shown to exist by the arguments against reductionism, assuming those arguments are sound.

I go so far as to speculate that such a social relation figures in testimonial justification in the manner just described. I am happy to say that the social relation here is in some sense an interpersonal relation. It involves at least whatever social relation must obtain when a subject hears, understands, and as a consequence believes a proposition asserted by another person. But this is evidently a weak interpersonal relation. I would allow cases of testimonial justification in which a subject comes to be justified on testimony by picking up a belief "from the air" without realizing anyone has provided testimony. The subject need not even be aware of a relation to another person. But I do not go as far as writers who claim that testimonial justification involves an interpersonal relation of assurance in which the subject gains justification for the belief in virtue of the testifier's offer of taking responsibility for the truth of the proposition, or in virtue of the subject's acceptance of such an offer. I have made a case against this assurance view in "The Assurance View of Testimony" (in Adrian Haddock, Alan Millar, and Duncan Pritchard, eds. *Social Epistemology*, Oxford: Oxford University Press, 2010, pp. 216-42).

A related question about testimony to which I have contributed is whether testimonial justification should be considered merely transmissional or generative. I have argued that testimonial justification is transmissional to the extent that memorial justification is so. This is an interesting question but a diminutive one. For even on the most extreme view of the generation of justification by testimony and its uptake, a testimonially justified belief can deviate from any of the propositions the actual or believed testifiers have reason to believe only in being derived by the subject via some justifying inference from a conjunction of these propositions. This is a very limited generation of newly justified propositions.

Collective Epistemology. In common speech we say that social groups of individuals, social institutions, and other collectivities believe, are justified in believing, and know things, as well as have intentions, desires, and other attitudes. In some cases, when we attribute group knowledge, we may have in mind no more than that all or most individual members of the group have knowledge. But in the more interesting cases, we think of the group as a plurality of individuals or as a single agent or subject, and we take this plurality or subject to have knowledge. I argued against treating group knowledge in this sense as a mere summation of the knowledge of members (in "The Justification of Group Beliefs," in *Socializing Epistemology*, Lanham, Md.: Rowman and Littlefield, 1994, pp. 257-87). Group knowledge in this sense is already social in a way different from any in which individual knowledge might be social: the subject who possesses the knowledge is social, in virtue of its collective character. But it is also true that the considerations I have already mentioned in favor of saying that social conditions figure in individual knowledge carry over to group knowledge simply because groups resemble individuals in their dependence on testimony and in their resources for deriving testimonial justification from non-testimonial sources. Of course, the interest of collective epistemology with regard to the overarching question of whether social conditions figure in knowledge will be greater if there are further respects in which group knowledge is social beyond those in which all knowledge must be social. In the paper most recently cited, I argued that there are such further respects in which group knowledge is social. I also argued that certain views proposed for individual justification are more plausible for group justification than others (notably, reliabilism is more plausible than coherentism). It is an interesting question what bearing this has on the plausibility of these views for individual justification.

There are other matters about group beliefs on which I have written. For example, social psychologists have shown that there is a pervasive phenomenon of social influence in persuasion: individuals are persuaded by others in accordance with whether they perceive themselves to belong to the same social groups as the others. It is hard to escape the view that this phenomenon degrades the epistemic status—justified belief or rationality—of the beliefs it affects. I have asked whether this degradation might nevertheless be compensated by a positive role for the phenomenon in the formation of rational group beliefs ("Rational Persuasion and Group Belief," *Fenomenologia e societa* 20, 1997: 66-93).

Recently there has been much attention to the question whether group belief or rational group belief might be identified with a complex aggregation of the beliefs of group members. Which aggregation functions have intuitively attractive properties? I am inclined to view this inquiry as relevant to the question which methods groups should employ to settle issues. But there must be a more basic phenomenon of group belief and rational or justified group belief than the one characterized in this way. A population's exhibiting in some way a particular aggregation function doesn't amount to a group belief or rational group belief unless there is a group agent or subject that uses a method of aggregation conforming to the function. And the use of a method itself depends on prior group beliefs. So these prior beliefs cannot be assumed to result from the use of a method of this sort, on pain of a regress of uses of methods. Moreover, if the use of a method is to produce a rational group belief, it must result from some practical group reasoning about which methods have desirable features. This prior group reasoning is not merely conformity to an aggregation function, nor can it be the use of a rational method of aggregation, on pain of regress. From these points I infer that there is a layer of group epistemology underneath aggregation as it is currently discussed. The topic of the justification of group beliefs I treated in my paper belongs to this layer.

Consensus. Individuals may disagree on an issue and recognize one another's disagreement. One can ask how the recognition of disagreement should affect their opinions: how far should an individual revise an opinion when confronted with the differing opinions of others? I contributed to the literature on Keith Lehrer's approach to the question, which requires averaging the subjective probabilities of the population, weighted by the degrees of respect each individual is assigned by all ("Consensus, Respect, and Weighted Averaging," *Synthese* 62, 1985: 25-46). The current literature on disagreement often assumes that

Lehrer is right that averaging is in order, and even weighted averaging when respect is properly assigned. The literature has focused on the prior question how to assign respect: should I give the probabilities of those regarded as peers equal weight with my own, or should I discount their probabilities on the basis of the character of the disagreement (e.g., the disparity in the probabilities, or finding the other's probability absurd) when I determine how far to revise? Rather than address these matters here, I will remark on the overarching significance of the question of revision in light of disagreement. The question is a sort of mirror image of the question of testimonial justification. In asking the latter question, we ask whether an individual having no opinion on an issue can come to be justified by adopting the opinion of another on the issue, and we ask just how such justification works. In asking the former question, we ask whether an individual having an opinion on an issue can remain justified without adopting or moving toward the opinion of another and just how far the individual must move to hold a justified opinion on the issue. There is, however, an asymmetry in the interest of the two questions with regard to their implications for how social justification must be. The question about testimony offers the prospect of an argument that the justification of individual beliefs is constituted in part by a social relation. For it offers the prospect of the argument, mentioned above, that the justification of an individual's belief on testimony depends in some cases on the justification of the testifier's belief. The question about disagreement offers no similar prospect of an argument that the justification of individual beliefs is constituted in part by a social relation. Suppose that when an individual disagrees with another, the individual must move toward the opinion of the other. No basis for thinking so presses us to conclude that after this revision the justification of the revised opinion is in some sense constituted by the justification of the other's opinion. The most plausible basis for thinking that the individual must move toward the opinion of the other is that the individual has reason to believe that before revision he or she is no more likely to have a correct opinion than the other, perhaps because he or she is no more likely to have sufficient reason for the opinion than the other is to have sufficient reason for the opposing opinion. When added to the reasons for the opinion the subject originally had before recognizing the disagreement, this reason for a belief about the relative likelihood of having a correct opinion may be enough justification for the revised opinion, and there is no pressure to think that this justification is constituted in part by the justification possessed by the other. In the case of testimony, the pressure to think that the subject's justification is constituted by the testifier's justification arises from the arguments against reductionism, which if sound show that the subject lacks a nontestimonial reason to believe, supplemented by the assumption that justification requires a reason to believe. But in the case of disagreement, the subject may very well possess a sufficient reason for the revised opinion quite independently of any reason the other has for the opposing opinion, in virtue of possessing a reason for thinking it no more likely that he or she has a correct opinion than that the other does. And if the subject does not possess such a reason, then there is no case that the subject must move toward the others' opinion, however well supported that opinion may be. Consequently, there is no case that, to avoid skepticism, we must take the subject to have as a reason for his or her opinion the reason the other possesses for an opinion on the issue. These points lead me to conclude that testimonial justification bears on the question whether individual justification is constituted by social relations in a way that revision in disagreement does not. In this respect, it is a more fundamental issue for social epistemology.

The History of Social Epistemology. Historians of philosophy have yet to devote much attention to the history of social epistemology. Some exceptions to this are C. A. J. Coady's treatment of the history of the epistemology of testimony in *Testimony: A Philosophical Study* (Oxford: Clarendon, 1992) and the contributions to the special issue of *Episteme* on the history of social epistemology, edited by Oliver Scholz and myself (*Episteme* 7, 2010: 1-99). My sole contribution to this area, apart from the introduction to that special issue (coauthored with Oliver Scholz), is a study of the role of consensus in Peirce's account of proper belief-fixing method in his famous article, "The Fixation of Belief" ("Justification and Consensus: The Peircean Approach," *Protosociology* 16, 2002: 241-286). On Peirce's account, justified beliefs (as we would call them) are correlated with consensual beliefs in a way to which we must attend when we evaluate or theoretically describe justified belief.

3. What is the proper role of social epistemology in relation to other disciplines?

I do not think that social epistemology provides any new reason to question a division of labor between a priori, conceptual, and normative epistemology, on the one hand, and empirical science, on the other. Whether there is such a division of labor must be settled, if at all, by debates in the philosophy of language, general epistemology, the general theory of norms, and now the foundations of experimental philosophy.

There are various ways in which social epistemology may rely on empirical findings. Consider, for example, an approach to knowledge that infers the content of the concept of knowledge from the function of that concept, or its application, in human life (as in Edward Craig's

Knowledge and the State of Nature). This approach is naturally as-signed to social epistemology because the function of the concept of knowledge in human life is plausibly in part a social function. Some a priori study and conceptual analysis would seem to be needed to iden-tify the concept of knowledge in enough detail to permit tracking its social function. And some a priori study would seem to be needed to establish that this sort of investigation is as likely to be fruitful as con-ventional conceptual analysis. But the question whether the concept of knowledge has a social function, and what social function it has, are substantially empirical questions, ones difficult enough to exceed the capacity of naïve observation and require the services of social science. Attempts to discover the content of concepts by empirical investigation are hardly new. Locke and Hume both endeavored to uncover the con-tent of concepts, or in some cases the emptiness of expressions of pu-tative concepts, by examining the psychological histories of ideas. This depends on a causal account of the content of concepts. Hume even had the notion that some concepts serve to refer to things other than their contents in virtue of how we employ those concepts in thinking. Hume's notion bears a family resemblance to the notion under discus-sion, of looking to the use of the concept in life to discover its content.

Craig proposes that the social function of the concept of knowledge is to identify good informants. I am sure that this is too narrow a view. The social function of the concept should include as well identifying agents who are able regularly to perform successful actions because they are able regularly to make the discriminations and form the true beliefs on which the success of those actions depends. Whichever view of the social function of the concept of knowledge is right, a full investigation of the concept by attention to its social function is bound to depend on empirical findings. This is not to deny that philosophers are the ones best positioned to initiate and organize such an investigation. For one thing, recent social science has not been especially friendly to the idea that cognitive items like concepts have determinate social functions with explanatory significance. It may be that philosophers will have to work to make the idea respectable to others. For another thing, suc-cess in this investigation depends on keeping one's eye on general and methodological issues, and on considering a wide range of options, and philosophers may be better positioned to do so than scientists focused on limited domains of inquiry. Success will depend on attention from many kinds of researchers, philosophers among them.

Whether the content of the concept is uncovered by conceptual ana-lysis or by empirical investigation, a well-supported assessment of whether the conditions of knowledge are satisfied may depend on the findings of social science. Whether a social account of knowledge will depend on such findings for its assessment of whether the conditions of knowledge are satisfied will turn on the details of the account. It cannot be ruled out in advance of uncovering the content of the concept that the social conditions mentioned in the account are so easy to judge that, although judging them is an empirical matter, no social science is needed. It seems unlikely but cannot be ruled out in advance that the concept of knowledge that serves a social function turns out to impose an accessibility condition according to which users of the concept must be able to tell from naïve observation unaided by science that the conditions are met.

4. What have been the most significant advances in social epistemology?

The field of social epistemology is only a few decades old. I would emphasize these advances. First, we have asked various questions scarcely entertained in previous epistemology, such as the ones I have mentioned above. Second, we have developed alternative epistemological accounts on many issues and revealed some of their relative strengths and weaknesses. Third, we have imputed some structure to the field. For the time being it is plausible to work with a tripartite division of the field into the study of the role of the social in individual knowledge, collective epistemology, and the epistemology of social arrangements, structures, activities, and processes. Fourth, we have learned to employ formal models and mathematical results to constrain the options for solutions to problems or to show that no solution having the desired characteristics is possible (as impossibility theorems about belief aggregation show). As the reader would expect from what I have said above, I regard questions in social epistemology as significant to the extent that they suggest views according to which social conditions constitute conditions of knowledge. I have indicated these issues above.

5. What are the most important open problems in social epistemology and what are the prospects for progress?

So immature is the field of social epistemology that I am inclined to say that, with the exception of some important though nonbasic issues resolved by mathematical proofs, all of its problems are still open and will remain so for the foreseeable future. So difficult are the tasks of judging our dependence on testimony and understanding the nature of social groups and group cognition that I do not expect decisive progress immediately in some main problems of social epistemology.

The most serious obstacle to progress in my view is that we lack empirical studies of how dependent on testimony our beliefs are. Do we or do we not possess sufficient nontestimonial beliefs on which to base beliefs about the reliability of testimony? Without guidance from careful empirical research, we cannot resolve the question of reductionism regarding testimonial justification. Another serious obstacle to progress is that we lack an understanding of the nature of group belief and reasoning. We have no developed metaphysics or philosophical psychology of group cognition or agency to rely on in accounting for group belief—nothing comparable to what we have in accounting for individual belief. Without such a metaphysics, we are bound to flounder in our attempt to account for group knowledge. This is one reason that I have looked into the nature of groups and specifically group beliefs ("Joint Action: From Individualism to Supraindividualism," in *Socializing Metaphysics*, Lanham, Md.: Rowman and Littlefield, 2003, pp.129-165; and "Group Belief and Acceptance," in Sara Chant, Frank Hindriks, and Gerhard Preyer, eds., *From Individual to Collective Intentionality*, Oxford: Oxford University Press, 2014). Similarly, despite the development of models from game and communication theory, we lack a firm understanding of dialogue and conversation. Without these we will not fully understand group justification, argumentation, or the process of justifying claims to an audience.

About the Editors

Duncan Pritchard, FRSE is Professor of Philosophy at the University of Edinburgh and Director of the Eidyn research centre. He works mainly in epistemology, and has published widely in this area. His books include Epistemic Luck (Oxford University Press, 2005), The Nature and Value of Knowledge (with A. Millar & A. Haddock, Oxford University Press, 2010), Epistemological Disjunctivism (Oxford University Press, 2012), and Epistemic Angst: Radical Scepticism and the Groundlessness of Our Believing (Princeton University Press, forthcoming). In 2007 he was awarded the Philip Leverhulme Prize. In 2011 he was elected to a Fellowship of the Royal Society of Edinburgh. In 2013 he delivered the annual Soochow Lectures in Philosophy in Taiwan.

Vincent F. Hendricks, is Professor of Formal Philosophy at the University of Copenhagen, Denmark, Elite Researcher of the Danish State. He is the author of many books, among them (Infostorms, Copernicus Books / Springer 2014), Mainstream and Formal Epistemology (Cambridge University Press, 2007), and The Convergence of Scientific Knowledge (Springer, 2001). He is also the author and editor of numerous papers and books in bubble studies, formal epistemology, methodology and logic. Hendricks is editor-in-Chief of Synthese and Synthese Library.

Index

Lightning Source UK Ltd.
Milton Keynes UK
UKHW041140291121
394778UK00001B/180

9 788792 130532